FRESH BREAD

How Jesus Draws Us to God

Douglas McMurry

WINEPRESS WP PUBLISHING

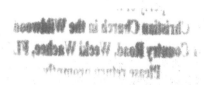

Printed in the United States of America

Packaged by WinePress Publishing, PO Box 1406, Mukilteo, WA 98275. The views expressed or implied in this work do not necessarily reflect those of WinePress Publishing. Ultimate design, content, and editorial accuracy of this work are the responsibilities of the author.

Unless otherwise noted, all Scripture quotations are from the Holy Bible, New International Version, Copyright © 1973, 1978, 1984 by the International Bible Society. Used by permission of Zondervan Publishing House. The "NIV" and "New International Version" trademarks are registered in the United States Patent and Trademark Office by International Bible Society.

PostScript is a registered trademark of Adobe Systems, Inc.

ISBN 1-57921-201-8
Library of Congress Catalog Card Number: 98-89783

Contents

To my parents, Elmer and Mitzi McMurry,
who first presented to me the aroma of Christ.

Acknowledgments

I am deeply indebted to Chris Walker for his invaluable suggestions in editing and shaping this book. Also to John Lindner for his beautiful cover, to Betsy Chalmers for computer imaging and typesetting, and to a bequest from Sadie Riedesel, my wife's mother, to help in the publication of this book.

I am also indebted to the support and encouragement of my friend, Brad Long, and the community of Presbyterian and Reformed Renewal Ministries International. In that community are two persons whom God used mightily to reawaken the Bread group vision and inspire the present book: Rev. Frank Drake and Hauke Powers.

—Douglas McMurry

The only book we recommend is
The Bible.
Read all others with discernment.

How To Use This Book

The way of Christ is not a head trip, but a spiritual pilgrimage into the first-hand experience of God. Most people find that this journey is best taken in company with a few others, for where two or more are gathered in Jesus' name, there He is in the midst of them. Besides, God calls us to learn love, and it is very difficult to love anyone when we remain by ourselves.

Therefore, the best way to use this book is in a group of three to twelve people. It is preferable for the group to have a leader or perhaps two (especially in groups of more than six people) who can keep the group on track.

I recommend that each member of the group make the following commitments to each other:

Three Basic Commitments In a Bread Group:

1. *We will all* make the BREAD group our social priority at the agreed time for the next twenty-two weeks (give or take a few weeks for vacations and holidays). If we can't make the group meeting, as a courtesy, we will call the leader in advance.
2. *We will all* do the reading and writing recommended between meetings.
    * Read the chapter and scriptures.
    * Write in a journal our responses to the Questions in the text, and our questions and reflections about the scriptures.
3. *We will all* use discretion in sharing what other people say in group meetings. These things may not be meant to be publicized outside the group.

I have written this book as a personal dialogue between myself and my reader. There are ***questions*** interspersed throughout the text that I invite you to ponder, even to write about in a prayer journal or diary. Let it be as though you and I were chatting with each other in a living room with a toasty fire. You will find these questions during small group meetings by looking for the "*Q*" in the margins.

There are also six *scriptures* at the end of each chapter, which I hope you will read in conjunction with the chapter itself. One way to do it is to read the chapter first, then on the six other days of the week, read one verse, and perhaps meditate on one of the questions. In this way, you are disciplining yourself to take time with God each day. I have added a one-sentence summary for each scripture selection, to help you remember what that passage says, during group discussions.

What You Will Need For the Journey

I recommend that you purchase *a Bible*—an NIV Study Bible, if you can afford it. The New International Version (NIV) is the version I quote from most often in my book.

Also, buy a *notebook or blank book* for a journal. In the journal you can write down your reflections about my questions, as well as any questions or thoughts that pop up during your reading of the scriptures. Often the questions *you* ask will make good material for stimulating group discussions.

Hopefully, you will find your Bread group a welcome combination of helpful ingredients that draw you close to God:

1. A few other people who sincerely want to know God

2. Biblical teaching that sticks to the basics (the *Fresh Bread* book)

3. A leader who is not manipulative or coercive, but who trusts the Spirit of God to be the main teacher.

Introductions

Maybe you are like me. Maybe you are where I was, at the beginning. I had grown up in a denominational church, but I had not found God there. So I was confused. And I was starving—starving, I tell you—for God. I was depressed, anxious, joyless, trapped in my thoughts, becoming more troubled with each passing day. I asked myself, *If God cannot be found in the place where He is supposed to be found, where, then, should I look for Him?*

At the beginning, I knew only this: There was a deep emptiness, a yawning vacancy in my life that produced discontent at the beginning of each day. I didn't know even what to call this emptiness, much less how to fill it. But my church had at least given me this: it had told me where to start my search: at Jesus and the Bible. So that is where I began my earnest inquiry after God. In this way, I saved myself much wandering and confusion.

Maybe you have never darkened the doorway of a church, and you are not so convinced that Jesus is the answer to people's spiritual searchings. But you are at least willing to look where I looked, as one of many possibilities, to see what is there. If you are as starved as I was, you can't afford to be choosy. You have to search wherever there is an aroma that promises bread to fill that emptiness.

Listen, my friend, I know what it is like, that void that makes you sad or at least unfulfilled every day of your life. You try to fill it with this or that, but nothing works. Nothing satisfies.

I was a miserable beggar once, never having enough of anything, and never satisfied. Now I am a rich man, with plenty of bread on my table. Now that I have what I need, I have become—as one saint used to say—"one beggar telling another beggar where the bread is."

Jesus is the Bread of Life, and I hope you find Him as I have, whether you are a "church person" or not.

—Douglas McMurry

O abide in the simplicity that is in Christ Jesus, in the naked truth that you have felt there! It is there that you will be able to know and distinguish your food, which has several names in Scripture but is all one and the same thing: the bread, the milk, the water, the wine, the flesh, and blood of him who came down from heaven. It is all the same food, only it is given to us in different measure—sometimes weaker, sometimes stronger—according to the capacity we have for receiving it. Thus, it is given different names.

—Isaac Penington

...e only book we recommend is
The Bible.
Read all others with discernment.

The targets we choose for ourselves are like the targets at a shooting gallery.

PART ONE

Receiving by Faith the Promises of God

1
A Purpose for Living

Sometimes the biggest questions are never asked. They are too big. We can't focus on them. I invite you to ponder just such a question now:

Q1: What is your life for?

Let me put it differently. Imagine that you contracted a fatal sickness today which put you on your deathbed. As you lay there in bed, reflecting on your life up to this point, would you be satisfied that you had lived it well? Or would you feel that you had wasted your life?—that, whatever the aim was supposed to be, you had missed it somewhere along the line? What, then, is your life for?

We All Have Targets

All of us have chosen targets toward which we aim our lives. Life is unbearable without a target. No one loves to wander aimlessly. But often, we choose our targets unconsciously. For many years I pursued targets without asking myself which ones were worth pursuing.

I remember some of my first targets. When I was in the fourth grade, my gym teacher would ridicule some of us kids in front of the class. His sneer threw me off balance. For the first time in my life, I believed that I was not as good as others. Soon I had a target: to prove to everyone that I could excel in the broad jump, or in running the football.

After discovering that my skinny legs would not support me in such endeavors, I switched my target to academics. By the fifth grade I could put together a better insect collection and write better nature study reports than most anyone at school.

In high school I decided that the true purpose of life was to be found in a professional career. An aptitude test had revealed that I might make a good art teacher. I had never taken an art course, but I believed in aptitude tests. Six years later I was ready to be an art teacher. But I still sensed an emptiness in my life. Teaching art was not enough to bring me fullness of life.

Yet I still believed in professions. I thought that I had simply chosen the wrong one. So I picked one that seemed to hold out more promise: the pastoral ministry. I had known pastors I had respected, and I thought that a theological school would train me in how to help people. I had not the slightest idea of what I wanted to help people to do. I just thought it would be a good thing to enter one of the helping professions. This was how I thought of the pastorate. Love for God had little to do with my decision at the time. Helping people was replacing academic achievement as my life's target.

While in seminary I added two other aims: marriage and family. Both, I thought, were essential if I were to be fulfilled. But aiming at several targets at once did not make my life more fulfilling—just more complicated. A part of me was still dissatisfied and empty.

I was bewildered. Had I not enjoyed every opportunity anyone could expect in life?—a good education and upbringing, perfect health (marred only by signs of an ulcer), a challenging professional calling, a beautiful wife and a free country? What more could anyone ask for? Yet I thought: if this is all there is, why do I feel so incomplete and dissatisfied—as though there ought to be something more?

Q2: Have you ever felt as though you have everything you could possibly want, yet something essential is still missing? Have you ever sensed a deep spiritual hunger that cannot be satisfied by all the little remedies your mother gave you against a blue Monday? To what do you attribute that sense of dissatisfaction or emptiness?

Spiritual Appetites

It is no trivial thing, this hunger. In fact, this is what drew me into the "bakery" of God, the Kingdom of Heaven, fresh with all its delights and aromas. Without that hunger, I should not have had the least interest in God for many years to come—perhaps never.

As for me, it was not fear of death or the hope of life after death that pulled me to God. It was this question about the meaning and purpose of life, my earthly life. At times my mind could hardly put this question into words—it just gnawed at my stomach like a rat, literally paining me. It melted there into a hunger for some life-purpose beyond the many I had already provided for myself. Why were my own targets not good enough for me? I hungered for something more. I think I was discovering that I have a spiritual nature.

Huge numbers of people at the turn of the millennium are discovering their spiritual nature, as I was during those years. One writer recently put it this way: "If you talk religion to us, we expect to receive a spiritual experience of the living God. We want, as a generation, to move beyond philosophical discussions of religions to the actual experience of God in our lives."[1]

Gone are the days of atheism and the universal faith in a godless science. Today atheism is out. There was something in it that shriveled people's souls. Today, three out of four Americans say that having a close relationship with God is very desirable.[2]

We search to fill an inner emptiness. Is this what Jesus meant when He said that we cannot live on bread alone, but on every word that comes from the mouth of God (Matthew 4:4)?

How does this relate to our search for a valid purpose for living? Could it be that God alone can give us our purpose for living? When we try to provide it for ourselves, our efforts fall flat. As the Bible puts it, our works are "burned up" (1 Corinthians 3:15). What is left at the end of the day? Is anything worth living for, that will not be burned up? How can we live our lives so that we will not *forfeit* them (Matthew 16:26), but *invest* them (Luke 19:13)?

Jesus, the Bread of Life

In 1972 I began to sense my mistake. Even while serving God by helping others, I had ignored God Himself. I had let a professional clergy career be my god. That this career had Christ's name attached to it only served to mask the masquerade more perfectly. Christian ministry is not the Bread of Life. Jesus is. The fruitful vine does not grow out of a professional career. It grows out of Jesus, who said, "I am the vine; you are the branches" (John 15:5).

Finally identifying where my emptiness was coming from, I searched desperately for Jesus. I cried out: "Jesus, are You there? If so, let me know you are real."

I began to read the Bible voraciously, as though my life depended on it. I wondered if its promises could become true for me— not just in theory, but experientially. Is Jesus really there with power? How can I know Him personally? Will He be my Bread of Life? Is it true what I read in the Bible?—

For we are God's workmanship, created in Christ Jesus to do good works, which God prepared in advance for us to do. (Ephesians 2:10)

Did God create me for a purpose, for special works He wants me to accomplish before I die? I decided the only way I could find out was by being "in Christ Jesus," by moving as close to Jesus as possible. This was for me a grand experiment: Try Jesus and see what would happen.

I now saw it: Jesus Himself is the Target. To Him I said, "Lord, I give my career to You, and my marriage and all the other targets I have accumulated. I'll even be a ditch-digger if that is where You want me. I just want it to be You, Lord, who draws me onward toward Yourself—if You are really there. Let me love You with all my heart. Won't You be my Target?"

The Best Decision I Ever Made

There! It was a decision, a trial experiment. I would step into what little I knew about Jesus, and see what might result. My years growing up in a church seemed now a shadow of something big that I was just discovering. I turned my attention from the shadow to the one who cast it. I would make it my aim to know God, because in Jesus and through His apostles, that is what God said He wants. Maybe, as I came to know Him, I could find out how He planned to spend my life.

This decision to give my life to God, in faith that He would receive and use it, has exploded my life, only to bring all the bits and pieces back together again in a new harmony. Above all, it has satisfied that deep inner hunger for meaning. It has given me an eternal purpose that does not sicken in time, leaving me on a sort of perpetual deathbed. Now, a quarter-century later, I do not remember a single day of regrets about that decision in 1972. Every year since then has been lived in deep satisfaction, even though there have been struggles, and things have not always gone as I expected or wanted. My experiment has yielded this conclusion: Jesus is the Bread of Life.

Getting Centered

I am a potter. On my potter's wheel is inscribed the pattern of a target. When I form pots on my wheel, the clay starts out lumpy and deformed. By disciplined effort I move every particle of clay until it is aligned to that bull's-eye on the wheel. We call this process "centering the clay." Until the clay is centered it cannot be made into a useful pot.

God spoke of Himself as a potter (Jeremiah 18:1-11). If He is to make useful vessels of us, we must first submit ourselves to the target on His potter's wheel. We must trade our targets for His Target. The only true wheel belongs to God.

The Apostle Paul had chosen a target: making a name for himself as a religious zealot. But when he discovered the surpassing worth of knowing and serving Jesus, he traded in his target for The Target (Philippians 3:4-11). He traded in all immediate claims for popularity and success, exposing himself to abuse and suffering. Yet he never regretted his decision. He had found the Center of the Universe. Everything else was a sideline compared to Jesus.

The targets we choose for ourselves are like the targets at a shooting gallery. You pay your money, take careful aim and shoot several times. With skill and luck, you hit the target. Yet as soon as you do, the target disappears. Your prize turns out to be a cheap kewpie doll stuffed with confetti. It looked better on the shelf.

Wrong Targets (Sin)

The Hebrew word for sin literally meant "to miss the mark." Sin is not only some evil deed we do for which we should feel guilty. It is something more serious, for behind our "sins" there lurks a deeper problem: a wrong mark or target. We are aimed away from God.

When I was in the tenth grade, I got it into my head to give my English teacher a hard time. I discovered that I could have the respect of my friends by teasing my teacher. I also took pride that I could tease him and still get A's on exams. All this was in violation of the golden rule. I did not do to him what I would have wanted him to do to me. But behind those sins of disrespect was a self-seeking ambition, tied to the drive for popularity and success that I had chosen as a target at the time. I had wrong targets.

The same type of thing happened in Jesus' day. Jesus showed that the religious people, who tried to avoid "sins," where just as lost as known sinners—corrupt politicians, prostitutes and pagans. Religious people, filled with envy and deceit, put Him to death. They thought they were right but they were blinded by sin: their own wrong targets. Many thought they were doing God a favor. Even people who don't think they are lost can be lost. Jesus, riding into Jerusalem, wept over them because they couldn't find God.

Q3: Do you see any evidence around you that people have lost their way and can't find God? Do you see any evidence of this in your own life?

The hunger for meaning and purpose is one of many spiritual hungers that God promises to satisfy in Jesus Christ.

Why spend money on what is not bread
and your labor on what does not satisfy?
Listen, listen to me, and eat what is good,
and your soul will delight in the richest of fare. (Isaiah 55:2)

In the next several chapters, I will tell about other ways that Jesus Christ can satisfy our deepest spiritual longings. My appetite for meaning and purpose was only the first that, I discovered, Jesus can fill with His bread of life.

Scripture Study for Chapter One

- **Ephesians 2:1-10** (The target of good works which God prepares in advance for us to accomplish)
- **1 Corinthians 13:4-14:1** (The target of love)
- **2 Corinthians 5:6-17** (The target of pleasing God)
- **Philippians 3:4-16** (The target of knowing Jesus)
- **Colossians 1:24-29** (The target of helping others become like Jesus)
- **1 Timothy 4:6-12** (The target of godliness—ordering every part of our lives to reflect a reverence for God)

The good shepherd lays down his life for the sheep.

2
Getting Right with God

People are searching for some solution to their spiritual hunger. So they search for God. They ask: "How can I know God?"

As an answer to this search, it is commonly said, "All religions are a search for God, and they all lead to the same God." This thought reflects a laudable distaste for arrogance. Western Christians have sometimes been arrogant, so it is an antidote to the mistakes of the past.

What Are the Main Entrees?

Yet when we view the religious foods listed on the menu, we find certain disappointments. The entrees sound fascinating, but what is brought from the kitchen turns out to be less than satisfying.

Let's begin with Hinduism. I quote from the late D. T. Niles, who, as an Indian Christian, described Hinduism from first-hand experience.

> Hinduism teaches that each man's religion is somewhere on the ladder of religious truth, and that no religion is false except when it claims to be the only and final truth.[1]

Hinduism is a philosophical system that accommodates everybody's god, and calls all of them collectively "God." In this system there is no distinction between truth and falsehood. Everyone's revelation or spiritual experience is given equal credence. Hinduism implies that no one really knows anything certain about God, therefore everyone's ideas are equally valid. By this line of reasoning, the Heaven's Gate cult, the Jim Jones cult, Mormonism, Buddhism, Islam, Judaism and Christianity are all equally valid, together with the teaching of every Hindu guru.

True, this approach lacks arrogance, and that is its appeal. But some of us have begun to sense that certain spiritual options are not benign, but are actually evil, and that we must make some attempt to sort through them. Hinduism fails to do this, defining "God" so broadly that the word no longer retains any definite meaning.

What About Buddha?

Buddhism came out of Hinduism as a reaction to some of the abuses and weirdness of paganism in India. My good friend, Brad Long, told of his experience of Buddhist temples he visited during his many years in Asia:

> Go to any active Buddhist temple. In the first courtyard you find images of many different gods. ...If you keep walking past the ornate, dragon-inlaid rooms into the outer courtyard, you come to a part of the temple with an entirely different atmosphere. Here, all is serene. You can see at the very back, amid calm dignity, a solitary plaque that says, *The Emperor of the Universe*. Nothing happens here. ...This emperor is so distant, he is all but obscured by the brass plaque that bears his name. ...All the attention in this Buddhist temple is directed toward other spirits who influence the daily lives of people.[2]

The answer of Buddhism to our search for God is this: "We don't know if God exists. If you have spiritual needs, try the other spirits. They will help you."

What of Islam?

Islam is the last of the major religious alternatives to arrive on the scene (7th century A.D.). Muslims describe their religion this way:

> ...The qualities and attributes which a man must possess, if he wants to pursue the way of Islam, can be cultivated and developed only out of profound knowledge of the attributes of God. It is the knowledge of God's attributes which purifies a man's mind and soul, his beliefs, morals and actions.[3]

This knowledge translates into a code of laws by which a person follows God and learns to please Him. To a Muslim, God is so high and unreachable that we cannot know Him in any personal way. We can only meditate on God's attributes and follow the code of laws He gave in the Koran.

Most Muslims, Buddhists and Hindus I have known are good and moral people. These religions, by and large, help people to follow moral ways. Of course, in every religion, including Christianity, there are some bad examples, and all of us would like to compare our "good apples" with someone else's "bad lemons." But that is not the point. We are asking a question: How can we know God? Are all religions pathways to the same God, and are they just different ways of knowing Him?

The answer we are sensing from the main religions is a rather disappointing one. None of the non-Christian options give us much hope that we could approach God Himself and get to know Him. The other religions seem to have bumped up against the inscrutable nature of God, the difficulty in knowing Him, and they offer other alternatives. They do help people to deal with their spiritual hunger, but not by helping them know God in any personal way.

Christianity, by contrast, says that God loves us and wants us to enter into a personal relationship with Him. In fact, that is why Jesus came. It is the only valid reason a person would become a Christian, and it is the aim of this Bread group to help people walk into this reality of *knowing God.*

Q1: Have you ever felt that God was distant and hard to get in touch with? Can you think of an instance when you tried to know God? Share with the group your own personal search for God up to this point in your life.

Jesus Spans the Great Abyss

The central belief of Christianity is that God came to us in Jesus, and that because of Jesus, God can be known in a personal way. Jesus is the Son of God, the perfect reflection of what God is like. Not only that, He has bridged the great abyss that separates us from God and makes God so inscrutable. How could this be?

According to Jesus Himself, Jesus did not come to us to be a good teacher. He came in order to die. Dying was what He had in mind all along. "For this purpose I have come" (John 12:27), He said,

referring to His own impending death. He said, "I am the good
shepherd. The good shepherd lays down his life for the sheep" (John
10:11). God sent Jesus the Shepherd to solve the problem of our
separation from Him. It is not by virtue of our actions, morality or
religion that we have a way to know God. It is by virtue of something
God did, to make this possible.

Love Creates Moral Order

To understand how this happened, we must try to see things
more from God's perspective than from ours. God loves us, or so the
Bible says. In His love for us, He has put us in a world where there is
order.

We could not survive without order. Order comes from God's
love. And a part of that order is moral righteousness and justice—the
sense of right and wrong that God has woven into the fabric of the
universe (Proverbs 3:19-20). All major religions have discerned this
moral order—though Western culture recently has been trying to
ignore it.

What would the world be like without moral laws? I am reminded of the sand-lot football games we used to play in my neighborhood. There were two types of football: "with ref" and "without
ref." When we had no referee to keep us honest, our games always
ended with fighting and bad feeling. But when one of our fathers was
willing to be referee, those games were more enjoyable. I now realize
that one of the most important people on the football field is the
referee. There could be no football game without him.

So in life, there could be no livable world without moral standards and enforcements. If we play by the rules and do not get side-
tracked by foul play, the "game" will be immensely enjoyable. But in
our sand-lot every player wants to win. Desperate to win, we commit
fouls. So God established penalties and ways to enforce them. Otherwise, there would be no justice, no peace, no order—*and no game!*
As in football, if no one ever got penalized, there would be no point
in having rules. The players would break them whenever it was to
their advantage to do so.

Yet how uncomfortable we are with rules, justice and morality. The very justice we require for our survival is the same justice that condemns us.

Coping With Condemnation

Condemnation. Truly an ugly word. Others do not have to condemn us: our self-condemnation is already more than most of us can handle. We try to cope with our sense of failure—usually by pushing the memory of it into oblivion and looking at ourselves in a more favorable light. The result? We lower our standards in that one area of conscience. We sympathize with ourselves and begin to redefine morality. Do I dare give an example or two? Maybe if I draw my examples from a generation ago, they will not seem so obnoxious.

In 1967, a study of parents of college age youth showed that 85% of Americans thought premarital sex was wrong. Most people called it "shacking up" or "living in sin." Twelve years later, a similar poll by the same organization showed that only 37% thought it was wrong.[4] We Americans have been redefining morality in the area of sex. Values we once held dear became too hard and cramped our individual freedom. Now psychologists, teachers and legislators from one end of the country to the other are trying to stop the epidemic of teen pregnancies, sexually transmitted diseases, single-parent families and unwed mothers.

Time magazine reported an epidemic of cheating on taxes and reported that it is "no longer kept secret but widely admitted, even joked about and accepted." The article concluded, "People who lie or cheat on their taxes are neither smart nor winners: they are simply cheats and liars."[5] True. But apparently most of us are cheats and liars.

Lying and cheating—the very words aggravate our guilt and make us angry that someone is probably trying to moralize us to death! Yet these are but two areas of moral integrity. Other areas may be equally obnoxious: adultery, gossip, temper, greed, lust, obscenity, unfaithfulness, bitterness—the list goes on and on, seemingly without end.

Q2: Are there any areas of your life where you see that standards you once held dear have been slowly eaten away?—that you have succumbed to a lesser vision than you once held? What feelings, if any, do you have about the loss of that purer vision and higher standards?

How We Hide from God

In the midst of all this, we hide from God, just as Adam and Eve hid from God in the Garden of Eden (Genesis 3:8). I have noticed this tendency often when I board an airplane, sit down next to a stranger and begin a conversation. All is well until the person asks, "What line of work are you in?" When I say, "I am a pastor," immediately I can spot that look on his face that says, "Oh boy, I got a man of the cloth here." For the rest of the trip, my seat-mate pretends to be asleep.

What is happening here? I believe that he is associating me with God, because he thinks of me as "a man of God." His contact with me brings up all sorts of unresolved issues with God. There is a chasm between him and God—and also, therefore, between him and me.

Much of this has to do with the way he has been living, which he is uncomfortable about, especially when he thinks about God. His way of coping with God is to run away. There is a gap, an abyss, between him and God, and that abyss is full of guilt. Like Adam and Eve, he has broken some of God's rules, he knows it, and so he avoids God. He may spend much energy justifying himself and trying to fend off the inner conviction that he is not fit company for God.

Condemnation.

Hunger Pang of the Conscience

Guilt is the hunger pang of the conscience. In Chapter One, I wrote of a hunger for meaning in life. Now I write of hunger for a clear conscience, for purity and goodness.

We have given up words like "adultery," "cheating," "lying," "gossip" or "fornication" because we are in process of admitting that faithfulness, honesty, discretion and sexual purity are impossible. We don't want to think about them any more. It is too painful to review our failures. Childhood innocence has given way to bitter reality. We know ourselves too well.

Now at last we are in position to see why Jesus died on a cross. God cannot redefine the boundaries and standards of righteousness that He, in His love, set up for us. These boundaries are our protection from moral chaos, which would engulf us with evil.

Jesus Himself, who reflects God's will and nature perfectly, recognized this. Consider, for example, His Sermon on the Mount, which is a summary of His most basic teachings:

> You have heard that it was said, "You shall not commit adultery." But I say to you that every one who looks at a woman lustfully has already committed adultery with her in his heart. If your right eye causes you to sin, pluck it out and throw it away; it is better that you lose one of your members than that your whole body be thrown into hell." (Matthew 5:27-29)

Whew! The Sermon goes on and on like that. People speak so glowingly of the Sermon on the Mount—maybe because it conveys so well that vision for truth, beauty and goodness we imagined as children. Yet no words seem quite so condemning as these.

The teachings of Jesus are not the answer to our self-condemnation. They are not the Bread for our conscience. They only show that God has not lowered His standards.

Bread for the Conscience

The death of Jesus is God's Bread for a tormented conscience. By suffering and dying, Jesus took upon Himself the penalty for our sin. He was temporarily forsaken by God, as the punishment for our wrongs fell on Him. God placed on Jesus the penalty we deserved.

> He was pierced for our transgressions, he was crushed for our iniquities. The punishment that brought us peace was upon him, and by his wounds we are healed." (Isaiah 53:5)

God knew what He had to do to remove the penalty that hung over our heads, and yet keep moral order intact. The death of Jesus was an *atoning sacrifice* to make us *at one* with God. God wanted to remove our shame and guilt, so that He could be friends with us, and we could know Him as deeply as He knows us (1 Corinthians 13:12).

But this could not happen without cost. God's reaching out was at the expense of the suffering and death of His beloved one.

The effect of this is to remove my reasons for hiding from God. Because of Jesus, I am justified. To say "I have been justified" means that in the eyes of God *it is just as if I'd* never sinned. God justifies me, therefore I don't have to justify myself before God.

Q3: Have you ever received assurance from God that your sin is forgiven? If so, share this experience with the group.

The apostle Paul summarized the effect that all this can have for us: "He who did not spare his own Son but gave him up for us all, will he not also give us all things with him? Who shall bring any charge against God's elect? It is God who justifies; who is to condemn?" (Romans 8:32-33).

How Martin Luther Came To Know God

Until we recognize this fact of history—the atoning death of Jesus—we tend to have a very grim idea of God. But hear this story of Martin Luther, who was released from years of self-condemnation when he discovered that he had been justified by God:

The whole of scripture took on a new meaning, and whereas before the "justice of God" had filled me with hate, now it became to me inexpressibly sweet in greater love.... If you have true faith that Christ is your Savior, then at once you have a gracious God, for faith leads you in and opens up God's heart and will, that you should see pure grace and overflowing love. This it is to behold God in faith: that you should look upon his fatherly, friendly heart, in which there is no anger nor ungraciousness. He who sees God as angry does not see him rightly but looks only on a curtain, as if a dark cloud had been drawn across his face.[6]

Q4: Is there anything that you have done that you need to release to God in order to be freed from an evil conscience? In a prayer journal or private diary list the main sins that trouble your conscience. Ask Jesus to give you assurance of God's forgiveness.

Scripture Study for Chapter Two

- **Genesis 22:1-18** (God asks Abraham to dramatize the future death of Jesus on Mt. Moriah 2000 years later)
- **Exodus 12:21-27** (Passover lambs presage the Lamb of God)
- **Isaiah 53** (A prophecy of the atoning sacrifice of Jesus for sin)
- **John 19** (The prophecy fulfilled)
- **Romans 8:28-39** (No condemnation for those who are called to follow God's Target)
- **Hebrews 10:11-25** (Christ's death provides permanent pardon once and for all)

On the other side of the ledger, Jesus became completely human.

3
How Jesus Portrays God to Us

If you or I were to offer our bodies on a cross to die a noble death, it is unlikely that God would view it as such a powerful act of love that the sins of other people would be wiped away because of it. What is it about Jesus' death that makes it so powerful in God's eyes? We must come to grips with the fact that Jesus was no mere human, but a totally unique being: God incarnate. God as a human being.

> He is the image of the invisible God, the firstborn over all creation.... For God was pleased to have all his fullness dwell in him and through him to reconcile to himself all things, whether things on earth or things in heaven, by making peace through his blood, shed on the cross. (Colossians 1:15, 19, 20)

Who Is This Jesus?

Paul plunges us into the real heart of Christianity here. If what Paul says is true, then all other claims made by anyone else pale by comparison. We must ask the key question, then: Who is Jesus?

There is no doubt that Jesus was a historical person. His presence in history is documented by Christians and non-Christians alike. For example, writing in 93 AD, the Jewish historian Josephus wrote:

> And there arose about this time, Jesus, a wise man, if indeed we should call him a man; for he was a doer of marvelous deeds, a teacher of men who receive the truth with pleasure. He won over many Jews and also many Greeks. This man was the Messiah. And when Pilate had condemned him to the cross at the instigation of our own leaders, those who had loved him from the first did not cease. For he appeared to them on the third day alive again, as the holy prophets had predicted and said many other wonderful things about him.[1]

Josephus, who was not a Christian, tells of Jesus' presence in history. The debate is not about *whether* Jesus was, but *who* He was and is. This question was illustrated recently when a team of Christians showed a *Jesus* film (a film tracing the life of Jesus from the gospel of Luke) at a Buddhist monastery:

> An itinerant JESUS film team managed to...get set up for a viewing in a famous Buddhist pagoda built upon an impregnable rock centuries earlier.
>
> At first the monks showed little interest. After all, they have their own tradition about Jesus: He came to one of the nearby Buddhist nations at age 12 and studied with the monks until he was 30! But as the film proceeded, one by one their attention was riveted on the story as they heard the gospel in their own language. At the film's conclusion, they exclaimed to one another that this story was different from the one they knew. They were so captivated by what they had seen and heard that they asked to see the film again! The team looked at one another, realizing they were witnessing one more instance of God's Spirit at work with the showing of the JESUS film. Regretfully, they replied they did not have enough gas for the generator. Undaunted, the monks went out and bought fuel themselves. After the second viewing, 37 monks prayed to receive Christ at this sacred Buddhist site built on solid rock![2]

The Buddhists had been taught one thing about Jesus. The gospel of Luke said another. When they heard the gospel of Luke, something happened to those monks to convince them that they had been wrong about *who Jesus is.*

God Made His Plans from the Beginning

Jesus' death was an effective atoning sacrifice not because it was noble and loving, but because Jesus was and is the Son of God, who was with the Father from before the Creation of the world. God planned this death from ancient times as a way of releasing people from the wages of sin—death and permanent separation from Him.

I find it especially intriguing that God began to reveal this death long before it happened. This is not, in other words, a doctrine dreamed up by Jesus' disciples to put a brave face on the death of their teacher. The incarnation of Christ—God becoming a man to die an atoning death—was revealed 2000 years before it happened.

For example, God reached into the life of Abraham, patriarch of the Semitic people. God asked him to sacrifice his son, Isaac, at the place of God's choosing. God then led Abraham to Mount Moriah, to the very place where Jesus would die 2000 years later, to enact a little drama (Genesis 22:2). Abraham didn't know it was a drama. He thought God was asking him to kill his son, though the request did not fit with what he knew of God. In the end, God provided a ram, and told Abraham to sacrifice it instead.

What was the point of this drama? God was revealing to Israeli culture a redemptive analogy—a model that would help people later on to understand how He was going to sacrifice His only Son as an atoning sacrifice for our sin. He wanted Abraham to walk with Him through His loss, to understand the depth of His fatherly love. "For God so loved the world that He gave His one and only son, that whoever believes in him shall not perish, but have eternal life" (John 3:16).

Revelations to Other Cultures

If God loves all people everywhere, and this sacrifice was intended to heal His relationship with all people, then you would expect God to reveal it to many cultures, not just to one. And He has! But His communications to diverse cultures about Jesus are still among the best kept secrets of history. For example, somewhere around 2000 B.C., God spoke into the Indian culture about His plans. The oldest Hindu writings, the Vedas, were written at a time when priests offered animal sacrifices, very much as the Hebrews used to do, and before any belief in reincarnation had emerged. These sacrifices came from the Indians' awareness of sin.

In recent centuries, Indians have believed that people must pay for sin by being born, again and again, into a world of suffering and pain. Reincarnation (through the transmigration of the soul) says that we have to pay for the sins of a previous life by suffering in our present one. If you are suffering, there is nothing that can be done for you; you are just getting what you deserve from a previous life.

But originally in India this philosophy had never been heard of. Indians believed that you could pay for sin by offering sacrifices. During that earlier time, some remarkable prophecies came forth, that God would one day offer a sacrifice for sin once and for all:

If one has to be delivered from all kinds of sins, such as sins committed through hearing, seeing, sinful thoughts, sinful deeds, sinful ideas, and sinful conduct, shedding of blood is necessary.[3]

The one who rules the world in order to atone for the sins of many allowed His body to be crushed and offered as a sacrifice.[4]

The Incarnate will be born to a virgin in a cattle shed.[5]

God loves Indian people. He has been preparing their culture for a long time to understand that He was sending a sacrifice for sin. Getting free of the burden of sin is not something you and I can accomplish on our own—no matter how hard we try. It is something God has done of His own initiative, and He wants us simply to understand it and accept it.

Some people think that Christianity is just the religion of European culture, "the white man's religion." It is true that white people have carried Christianity far and wide, and many have made mistakes as they have done so. But God has had His own ways of communicating the Incarnation of His Son, that transcend any one culture. God loves all cultures and all people, and He can communicate directly into any culture about Jesus.

For example, God brought three Parthian magi (astrologers) to worship the infant Jesus at the time of His birth (Matthew 2:1-12). Of course, these men had become aware of the prophesies of Daniel, which said that a king would come during the Roman empire, the fourth great empire from the reign of Nebuchadnezzar. Daniel actually prophesied the year Jesus would ride into Jerusalem and offer Himself as an atoning sacrifice for sin (Daniel 9:24-27). God confirmed His word among these magi by somehow communicating to them through their own culture that the King had been born according to promise, so they came to worship Him.

In 1740, a similar prophecy happened among the Coeur d'Alene people of Idaho. Chief Circling Raven received a prophecy that a savior had been born into the world as a baby many years ago. He introduced this message to his people. According to the Coeur d'Alene chief and historian, Joseph Seltice, the Coeur d'Alenes began to celebrate Christmas in 1740, long before any Christian missionaries or white people arrived on the scene.[6] Most of the other tribes of the Pacific Northwest received similar prophecies about the Savior during the 18th and 19th centuries.[7] They learned to call Him the Master of Life, because they didn't know His name.

How Can We Be Sure Jesus Is the Son Of God?

The scriptures of the Bible are by far our most reliable source of information about what God was doing through Jesus. I quote the others only to show how God's love knows no bounds. The Bible is a great treasure chest compared to the few pearls God has scattered into other cultures that are searching after God.

The Bible mentions several ways God provided testimony about who Jesus is. These are listed by the apostle John in John 5, for, as Jesus Himself said, "If I testify about myself, my testimony is not valid" (John 5:31). But God provided other testimony. According to John 5:39, the Old Testament provides testimony about Jesus in passages like this one:

> He said to me, "You are my Son,
>   today I have become your Father.
> Ask of me,
>   and I will make the nations your inheritance,
>   and the ends of the earth your possession. (Psalm 2:7-8)

In Matthew 3:16, we learn that God Himself confirmed that this scripture applies to Jesus. He said, "This is my beloved Son."

John the Baptist was a dynamic prophet who was widely recognized among the Jews to be a man of God, speaking God's truth. John also testified about who Jesus was (John 1:29-35).

The miracles Jesus did were a form of testimony (John 5:36). So was the power of Jesus' word, which was so authoritative that even demons had to obey it (Mark 1:27, John 5:36).

These were the reasons the apostles found it credible to believe that Jesus is the Son of God. In addition, God is able to provide a "testimony" about Jesus through the Holy Spirit from generation to generation since those days (1 John 5:9-12). In other words, the Holy Spirit bears witness in our hearts that Jesus is the Son of God.

Fully God, Fully Man

The ancient Christian creeds, whose purpose was to guard the teaching about who Jesus is, insisted that Jesus was at once fully God and fully human. Those early church councils, like the council of Nicea, are often portrayed as unimportant exercises in hair-splitting by old men who lived long ago and were out of touch with reality.

Not so. Many sects, cults and religions have come and gone, trying to come up with more reasonable and understandable ideas about Jesus. But I believe that God wants us to understand that Jesus was completely human and completely divine, both at once—a bridge between two worlds, God's and ours. It was necessary that Jesus be fully God (a perfect sacrifice not marred by sin) in order to be the required atonement for human sin. He needed to be fully human, so that His sacrifice would apply to humans.

Jesus was a totally unique individual, the God-man. There has never been anyone else like Him. "There is one God, and one mediator between God and men, the man Christ Jesus, who gave himself as a ransom for all men" (1 Timothy 2:5).

Jesus the Bridge between God and Us

This teaching has grown on me, and with each passing year, as I muddle through my sins and problems, I rediscover it at deeper and deeper levels with increasing appreciation. Jesus alone speaks with the authority of God, and also with sympathy from His human experience, both at once. He is therefore in a unique position to help me find my way to God, and He uniquely deserves to be followed and obeyed.

On the one hand, He knows more than any mere human being knows, because He is God. He is the image of the invisible God. He portrays God perfectly, in a way that no one else has ever done. On the other hand, He understands my human frailties and vulnerability, and treats me with understanding and compassion.

If Jesus were not fully God, the command, "Follow Me!" would lack clout. Other voices would have equal authority, and my life would become cluttered with good advice from a hundred gurus, professors, philosophers and TV personalities. On the other hand, if Jesus were not fully human, I might fall away because of discouragement, believing that God could never understand my struggles.

The One from Above

Jesus was "the One from above." "The one who comes from heaven is above all." Everyone else "is from earth" and "speaks as one from the earth." (John 3:31). Jesus spoke with an almost frightening authority that had nothing to do with Hillel, Gamaliel, Shammai or any other of the ancient Jewish "authorities" (Matthew 7:29).

The words of Jesus had an edge to them. They forced people to confront themselves, their lifestyles, their rationalizings: "What does it profit a man to gain the whole world, but lose his own soul? For what can a man give in exchange for his soul" (Mark 8:36-37)? Jesus spoke as God, correcting the entire human race, challenging us to look at ourselves as God looks at us. In this He is unique. He is the only one in human history who brings "testimony from above."

Jesus' teaching did not amount to words alone. The words had to be demonstrated, shown to be true. If Jesus said, "Do not be afraid of those who kill the body, but cannot kill the soul," well then, let Jesus submit Himself to the fire of persecution, be placed bodily on a cross to die like a criminal—and then let's see what happens. Let Him be the exhibit to show that His words are true. Let Him be the Pioneer, the first to penetrate the Doorway into Life, the firstborn from the dead.

Jesus reveals divine thinking not only in His teaching, but in His very life, His person. He *is* the Word of God. By nature He reveals divine love, divine holiness, divine character and divine reasoning.

Q1: Do you have any difficulty believing that Jesus was truly God, the Son of God, reflecting perfectly God's very nature? Is there anything He said or did that does not seem divine or perfect?

Yet He Was One of Us

On the other side of the ledger, Jesus became completely human. He had to suffer the burden of an outer nature—a body and a psyche—to endure stress, temptation, frustration, fatigue and death. During His time on earth, His energy and time were as limited as ours.

This fact is enough to explain why Jesus often asked the people He healed not to tell anyone about their healing (though there were probably other reasons, too). He simply had not the energy to minister to thousands of sick people all at once. Though He was full of the Holy Spirit (Acts 10:38), and all the compassion of God filled his heart (Matthew 10:36)—yet He was merely one of us (Hebrews 2:17). Jesus understands stress, tiredness, grief, weakness, schedules, conflict and temptation. He understands!

Q2: Do you accept the idea that Jesus was a person like ourselves, or do you see Him as a sort of Superman, who couldn't possibly understand your stresses and frustrations? Can you sense the human sympathy of Christ, as Hebrews 4:14-16 describes?

Jesus Has Authority To Speak

There is an everyday relevance to this understanding of Jesus as the Divine-and-Human-One. The early church leaders saw it, and that is surely why they gave their lives to preserve this teaching for us. They wanted us to have the true perception of who Jesus is, because without it, we cannot properly gain access to God. If we are hiring a guide for a journey, we would want him to know more about the way ahead than our next door neighbor does.

Suppose I meet an attractive woman, not my wife. I have an impulse! How shall I evaluate it? I have always followed traditional values. Maybe now is a good time to start following nontraditional values. I have read numerous books that tell me not to stifle or repress my sexual libido. "Let us liberate ourselves from the harmful moralistic attitudes of our Puritan and Victorian forbears," they say.

Now I picture two frowning people dressed in black, who shake their finger with one hand and hold a pitchfork with the other. These are my Puritan and Victorian forbears. They are trying to keep me from having a good time. Maybe at long last, I should repudiate them, join the sexual revolution and be one of those happy, self-actualized people who enjoy The Good Life.

Who is right?—sexual revolutionist or puritannical Victorian?

Neither. Jesus alone has clear vision. He knew human nature, yet His vision was not obscured by it. And this is what He said: "Anyone who looks at a woman lustfully has already committed adultery with her in his heart" (Matthew 5:28).

This may not be the answer I wanted to hear, but at least it is a clear answer, and I sense its truth. Jesus is going beyond tides of opinion here. His word is not oatmeal. He is warning me about how I relate to women other than my wife. A part of me, my inner nature, resonates with this answer. Jesus has given me a bit of heaven in this answer. He is not helping me justify myself, but preparing me for eternity with God. My other friends tell me what I want to hear, because that is what *they* want to hear. Jesus tells the truth, with authority.

He is the God-man.

Q3: Do you tend to think of Jesus either as more human than divine, or more divine than human? Why?

Q4: If Jesus is a perfect portrayal of God, how does He affect your picture of what God is like?

Scripture Study for Chapter Three

- **Colossians 1:15-20** (Jesus, the perfect expression of God's nature)
- **John 1:1-14** (Jesus, the Son of God, came to earth to show us God)
- **John 3:31-36** (Jesus is unique: He is the only "one from above")
- **Hebrews 4:14-16** (Jesus our high priest sympathizes with our human struggles)
- **Hebrews 2:5-18** (Jesus became fully a man to taste human weakness and death)
- **Philippians 2:5-11** (Jesus' transition to human nature was complete. He was no Superman)

Jesus was showing me that He is not dead, but very much alive.

4
Rescue from Destruction

Jesus' incarnation and death were not an end but a beginning. After Jesus died on a Roman cross, the Father then raised His Son to life on Easter morning. Jesus' empty tomb was the first inkling that Jesus was not destroyed by the death inflicted on Him. This initial evidence was confirmed several times as Jesus Himself met His disciples and interpreted for them what God had done.

Q1: Many of us celebrate Easter each year, yet are quite foggy about what we are celebrating. Why not put it into words: What meaning and importance does Easter have for you?

In the Bible, Easter gathers together three promises so wonderful that any one of them, to a Christian, makes Christ's resurrection the turning point in history.

A New Body Like His

To begin with, Jesus was "the firstborn from among the dead" (Colossians 1:18). He is not the only one to be raised from the dead, only the first. If Jesus received a new body—in Paul's words, a "spiritual body"—so will all who follow Jesus.

But our citizenship is in heaven. And we eagerly await a Savior from there, the Lord Jesus Christ, who, by the power that enables him to bring everything under his control, will transform our lowly bodies so that they will be like his glorious body. (Philippians 3:20-21)

The body we have now is like a seed planted in the ground, which some day will produce a "plant"—a "spiritual body." It is not God's will to leave our souls bodiless.

The body that is sown is perishable, it is raised imperishable; it is sown in dishonor, it is raised in glory; it is sown in weakness, it is raised in power; it is sown a natural body, it is raised a spiritual body. (1 Corinthians 15:42-44)

Nobody knows exactly what a "spiritual body" is. Nobody understands what Jesus' resurrection body was like. But we do have evidence that Paul was not having an imaginative or psychedelic experience when he spoke of it. The resurrected Jesus was seen at one time by five hundred disciples (1 Corinthians 15:6). Any notion that the resurrection of Jesus was only a myth or a dream must come up short against this evidence. Paul could never have gotten away with writing such a thing if it had not been a verifiable fact. Many of those disciples were still alive at the time he was writing. Paul did not have centuries of intervening time to spare him the embarrassment of people checking up on his facts. To publish wild, off-the-wall statements would have murdered his credibility, just as it would today.

Moreover, Paul does not strike us as one given to hallucinations or exaggeration. He was one of the great intellectuals of his day. To anyone who weighs credibility, Paul is credible. And he is telling us that a spiritual body, though mysterious, is quite real. And what is past history for Jesus becomes future hope for us.

If our "spiritual body" is like that of Jesus, then it will probably have these characteristics:

- It will be more than a disembodied soul.
- With the new body, we will be recognizable for who we are.
- It will not be as limited and limiting as the present one.
- It will not be subject to sickness and death.

This spiritual body is not promised to us until a time in the future—"at the last trumpet." At this time Jesus will return to earth with a cry of command with all His holy angels, to bring the earth out of its "bondage to decay" (Romans 8:20-22). All in God's time. However, there is a more immediate promise that will take place as soon as we die as believers.

The Salvation of Our Souls

The second promise of Easter was proclaimed by the apostle Peter: "...for you are receiving the goal of your faith, the salvation of your souls" (1 Peter 1:9). We often hear this word, "salvation." What does it mean?

Paul wrote: "For if, when we were God's enemies, we were reconciled to him through the death of his Son, how much more, having been reconciled, shall we be saved through his life!" (Romans 5:10). Saved from what? Paul adds: "from God's wrath."

You cannot avoid it: Paul has to be talking about hell. Now, what do you picture when you think of hell? Scary little red men with tails, horns and hooves running around in long underwear, jabbing people with three-pronged forks? Of course, this is silly, like a children's Halloween prank. I am convinced that most people get their ideas about hell from comic strips.

But Jesus spoke of hell as a real outer darkness:

> Many will come from the east and from the west, and will take their places at the feast with Abraham, Isaac and Jacob in the kingdom of heaven. But the subjects of the kingdom will be thrown outside, into the darkness, where there will be weeping and grinding of teeth. (Matthew 8:11-12)

Hell is an eternal separation from the loving presence of God, who invites us to a wedding banquet. Every Christian is invited into the presence of God from the moment we accept Christ as our Lord and Savior, and at death we enter into God's presence. For example, Jesus promised this to one of the thieves crucified with Him: "Today you will be with me in paradise" (Luke 23:43).

Paul wrote: "I desire to depart and be with Christ, which is better by far; but it is more necessary for you that I remain in the body" (Philippians 1:23-24). Paul was torn between two blessings: the purposeful work God had given him in this existence, and the eternal salvation God offered him in the next.

Q2: How do you feel about the prospect of your own death? Can you talk about it as freely as Paul did? Can you be as noncha-

lant or confident about it as Paul was about his? Have you ever faced imminent death (as Paul did)?

Rescuing Power

Hidden in this word "salvation" there is yet a third promise that shines through the Easter morning sun. Because of Easter, Jesus lives with power to rescue us in this life, when it suits His loving purposes. Salvation doesn't mean only "eternal life" in the future. It also means that Jesus is alive and has power to rescue us today.

I used to be skeptical about this sort of thing. As a student I was led to believe that if we are going to be saved from our problems, we have to do it ourselves. God has given us brains to "work out our own salvation," and "God helps those who help themselves."

Sometimes, to defend this point of view, I heard people quote these words: "Work out your own salvation with fear and trembling" (Philippians 2:12). But later I realized they misunderstood Paul's meaning. The Philippian church was having problems. When Paul wrote, "work out your own salvation," he meant that they did not have to always rely *on Paul* to solve their problems (in this case, the tensions among church members). They should recognize that God is available to help them in his (Paul's) absence, because Paul was in prison, and couldn't help them. In this case, "salvation" does not mean "eternal life," but "rescue from difficulties." Paul wanted those Christians to learn to rely on the rescuing power of God.

Everywhere in the Bible, we see how God wants us to learn how to rely on "his incomparably great power" which is "like the working of his mighty strength, which he exerted in Christ when he raised him from the dead..." (Ephesians 1:19).

This is so very different from what I learned as a child. When people said, "God helps those who help themselves," to me it was just a nice way of saying that God never really helps you. And if God never helps you, the only recourse you have in times of trouble is the wisdom of the helping professions.

Armed with this attitude, I decided to enter one of those professions. I learned many skills for helping people out of their problems: counseling, social work, political action and small group dynamics.

The gospel of Jesus was okay if you were concerned about life after death. But if it was *this* life you were concerned about, these skills were what you needed to rescue you from your problems.

Of course, these skills do help people. But if there is anything I have learned from nine years of higher education and thirty in the Christian ministry, it is the limits of human powers—at least, the limits of *my* powers. The conviction that I had to rescue myself from all my problems, and then, as a pastor rescue everyone else from theirs, led me to the brink of severe anxiety and personal despair.

Try an Experiment: Trust God

After I surrendered my life to God (as I described in Chapter One), I began to look to God to do things for me. A scripture had leapt out at me: "Anyone who comes to God must believe that he exists and that he rewards those who earnestly seek him" (Hebrews 11:6). Putting my confidence in the second part of this passage, I began to believe that God could reward me in tangible ways.

At the end of my first position as an ordained minister, I had to look for a new church. I had been a worry-wort for years, and had even developed signs of an ulcer. Something in me wanted to worry about this step into the unknown, too—to follow the old and familiar routine of sleepless nights and stomach pain. Yet I kept telling myself, "God is in charge, and He will take care of me." So every day I gave my insecurities to the Lord and asked Him to lead me.

It was a major turning point in my life. I was handing over control to Him, and asking Him, in return, to care for me. I was ready to look to Him to guide me to a new church, or—what? My future was a blank sheet, and I was saying to God, "fill it in as You see fit." The most immediate "salvation" in this decision was an almost miraculous release from a life-long habit of worry.

Beyond that, here is what God did to show me that I could rely on Him. He used Dick Lin, a former Buddhist who had been one of the first to embrace Christ as a result of my ministry. At that time, Dick had an inner awareness that God was going to take him to another town soon. A few months later, he lost his tenure as Professor at Oregon State University and moved to Hillsboro, Oregon, where he attended worship on the very Sunday that Hillsboro Presbyterian

Church was discussing how to hire a pastor. Through a long series of "God-incidences" the position was offered to me. And during my time of waiting for all this to be worked out, I had the distinct assurance that this position was going to be given to me.

This was my first clear experience of learning to trust God with the affairs of my life. Jesus, "who has all authority in heaven and on earth," was showing me that He is not dead but very much alive.

Q3: Do you believe in such a power in the world today? Have you ever seen any evidence of it? Write down the specifics in your prayer journal or diary, and share with your group.

If He Did It for Me...

Armed with this fresh conviction that God is actually there to rescue people, I began to share this good news with others. It became a major feature of my ministry in my new church at Hillsboro.

Ruth, the mother of one of our church members, called me late one night. She had been an alcoholic for at least a decade, and a resident of alcoholic wards much of that time. I had seen many such people during a year of social work training in a psychiatric hospital in Scotland. I knew how difficult it is to achieve lasting release from this bondage. Ruth had already sustained much liver and brain damage from her habit. Now she was asking me to tell her how she might be freed from this alcoholic prison.

Referring this woman to a psychiatrist was out of the question— she had been under psychiatric care for years. With her, there had to be another answer. I helped her look to Jesus, to rely on the Lord as her strength, and to see that she was in a prison from which Jesus could free her. She clung to this hope like a life raft.

One day, she locked herself in her apartment, together with her Bible, a tape of a sermon and Christian praise music. She was determined to seek God for salvation from alcohol, and not to come out of her apartment until He had saved her. And He did!

Jesus saved Ruth from alcoholism on the third day of her vigil. Doctors confirmed that her liver and brain were healed, too. She became a new woman, freed from alcohol for the rest of her life.

"Just a fluke," you say? Millions of people have experienced the saving power of Jesus Christ. Consider this personal story from former U.S. Senator Harold Hughes, who struggled with the same problem Ruth did:

> I am a recovered alcoholic. Twenty years ago, I'd hurt everyone and everything that I loved, and decided to take my own life. In desperation, with tears streaming down my face, I prayed probably the only honest prayer I prayed in a decade: "God help me; I cannot help myself. If there is any purpose in me living, you'd better show me 'cause I don't want to go on and I will not much longer." I knew at that moment God would help me to survive, and He did. It's up to us to make a decision. Either God's word is truth, or it is a farce. Either it's a living way of life, or simply a set of traditions that an atheist can do just as well. And if Jesus Christ isn't a personal Savior, if He didn't give us the Comforter to live in our hearts, then why go around pretending? But I know that God is alive. I know that Jesus Christ paid for my sins on that cross and set me free.[1]

True, Jesus does not always meet us in such dramatic ways. But when we give ourselves to Him, He is so very eager to fulfill His promises in us. And among those promises is His rescuing power.

Q4: Is there any area of your life where you see a need for Jesus to rescue you? Why not ask Him, and ask your group to pray for you in that area.

Scripture Study for Chapter Four

- **Romans 5:6-11** (Justified by His death; saved by His life)

- **1 Corinthians 15:1-28** (Jesus' resurrection; our resurrection)

- **Philippians 1:19-26** (A target for this life; a promise for the next)

- **Acts 3:1 - 4:12** (Rescue for a lame man)

- **Colossians 2:13-15** (Christ's victory)

- **Ephesians 1:15-23** (The power that raised Christ from the dead is available to Christians today)

Jesus said, "I am the bread of life…. And still you do not believe."

5
New Life: God's Bread

Jesus said, "I am the bread of life. He who comes to me will never go hungry, and he who believes in me will never be thirsty. But as I told you, you have seen me and still you do not believe. (John 6:35-36). Later He added, "I have come that they may have life, and have it to the full" (John 10:10), This "life" is an inner love, joy and peace that flow from the presence of God. Some have called it "glory." In Greek the word is *zoe* (ZOay).

Eternal Life

According to the Bible, this *zoe* life has several characteristics. To begin with, it is indestructible and eternal, "kept in heaven," a quality of life promised for certain people after we die. Jesus said, "I go to prepare a place for you" (John 14:2). He spoke of heaven as a place whose main feature is God's loving presence, which exudes "life."

My good friend, Brad Long, whom I have known for several years, had the following vision of heaven at about 11 p.m., March 21, 1998. I quote only a small part of a long visionary experience that caught Brad up into the heavenly realms and exposed him to God's love:

I was walking into the vision of the heavenly city of the book of Revelation. It was real, and I was really there! I felt this vast city all around me. I could just catch glimpses of fantastic architecture, but nothing very clear. I knew that what I was seeing were like caricatures formed in my brain as I was overwhelmed by a reality too vast and complex to comprehend. So I could tell you nothing of its actual appearance, only that I was there and that it was intensely real. A whole universe was flooded with the presence and joy of God and was inhabited by angels and people. I was aware of lush jungle-like vegetation, spectacular flowers, animals and wild, exuberant life, but nothing clear here. It was like the Ezekiel vision of the abundance of life on either side of the river of life (Ezekiel 47).

Then I saw the river. I felt the river rushing through me; it was the river of life. It was pure life, life abundant, overflowing, more real, more wonderful, and more alive than anything imaginable. It was in the city, and its inhabitants were in it. The river rushed like a thousand Amazons out into the created universe.

Then I was in the presence of Jesus again. His brilliance overwhelmed me, and I felt like I was going to explode from the inside because of the intensity of His love and presence. I heard him in my whole being say, "Go and bring my people into my city and into my river of life![1]

William Tennent

This sort of experience has been bestowed on a few people in the past, especially during seasons of spiritual awakening. For example, one Christian during the Great Awakening of 1740, William Tennent, was caught up to heaven while doing his theological studies at "The Log College" (later, Princeton Seminary). The experience was so holy, so precious to him, that he could hardly be persuaded to describe it:

While I was conversing with my brother on the state of my soul, and the fears I had entertained for my future welfare, I found myself, in an instant, in another state of existence, under the direction of a superior being, who ordered me to follow him. I was accordingly wafted along, I know not how, till I beheld at a distance an ineffable glory, the impression of which on my mind it is impossible to communicate to mortal man. I immediately reflected on my happy change, and thought,—Well, blessed be God! I am safe at last, notwithstanding all my fears. I saw an innumerable host of happy beings surrounding the inexpressible glory, in acts of adoration and joyous worship; but I did not see any bodily shape or representation in the glorious appearance. I heard things unutterable. I heard their songs and hallelujahs of thanksgiving and praise with unspeakable rapture. I felt joy unutterable and full of glory.[2]

Perhaps you question the validity of all such visionary experiences? Or perhaps you are ready to believe anyone who has an out-of-body or near death experience or vision? In relating these two experiences, I am only too aware of the possibility of counterfeit visions and even false teaching based on raw, untested experience. All such experiences must be checked against the revelation of God in the Bible, and none of us is obliged to believe everyone who claims to have "been to heaven." Still, the Bible says:

"No eye has seen,
     no ear has heard,
no mind has conceived
     what God has prepared for those who love him"—
but God has revealed it to us by his Spirit. (1 Corinthians 2:9)

Q1: Are these promises about eternal life in heaven important to you? Do you think much about them? If you took these promises more seriously, how might that affect your attitudes about your job, family and leisure activities?

Not Only for the Future

Some Christians have been so exclusively focused on the one promise of a future in heaven that they are unaware of the many other facets of this *zoe* life.

Let me tell a story of Madame Bilquis Sheikh to demonstrate how a person may experience *zoe* in the here and now. Bilquis, a Muslim woman in Pakistan, was drawn by her hunger for God to explore the promises of Jesus. According to her book, *I Dared To Call Him Father,* as a Muslim she did not believe that God could be known in a personal way. Yet as she began to inquire into Jesus, she began to enjoy a sense of God's presence with her. It took the form of an inner joy and peace, which she called "glory."

But then one day, she didn't feel like going to Sunday night Bible study. She made up an excuse and decided to stay home. Immediately, the glory of God left her. She didn't get it back until she asked God why His glory had departed from her, and recognized this lesson: "If you want to move forward with Me, you must not look for

excuses to avoid Christian fellowship. Christian fellowship is important." When she repented of her willfulness in avoiding Christian
fellowship, the glory returned. God was teaching her.

A few days later, she didn't get much sleep at night, so she decided not to have her morning quiet time and Bible study. After that,
she had a terrible day. God's ways were dawning:

> That was the second time when I seemed to be stepping out of the
> glory of the Lord's Presence.
>
> But the experience, nonetheless, left me with a strange sense of ex-
> citement. For I had the feeling that I was sitting on an important truth
> without realizing it. There were times when I was in the Presence and
> experienced that deep sense of joy and peace, and there were times
> when I lost the sense of His Presence.
>
> What was the key? What could I do to stay close to Him?
>
> I thought back over the times when He had seemed unusually
> close....
>
> And I thought about opposite times too, moments when I knew
> that I had lost this sense of His nearness. How did the Bible put it?
> *And grieve not the Holy Spirit of God (Ephesians 4:30, KJV).* Is that
> what happened when I scolded the servants? Or when I failed to
> nourish my spirit with regular Bible reading? Or when I just didn't go
> to the Olds' [for Bible study]?
>
> Part of the key to staying in His company was obedience. When I
> obeyed, then I was allowed to remain in His Presence.
>
> I got out my Bible and searched in John until I found the verse
> where Jesus says:
>
> *When a man loves me, he follows my teaching. Then my Father will
> love him, and we will come to that man and make our home within
> him (John 14:23).*[3]

One lesson Madame Sheikh was learning was that the promises
of God and the commandments of God go together. They are linked
together in the way of the New Covenant—a life of cooperation with
God. I will have more to say about this as we go along.

**Q2: Have you ever experienced the glory or "life" of God's pres-
ence as Bilquis Sheikh described it? Have you then experienced the loss of that presence? Try to remember a definite**

experience to share with the group. Is the glory or "life" that flows from God's presence worth seeking after?

The Search For Fulfillment

We all search for fulfillment. Most of the social and political movements of history have grown out of this search. Most of these movements assume that fulfillment is a goal we must strive after for ourselves. If we are willing to put out the effort, and if other people do not trample on our human rights, we may, with luck, attain it. But how easily this fulfillment is smashed by the harshness of this world.

The Bible casts a completely different light on this search for fulfillment. Was the Apostle Paul striving for fulfillment when he risked his neck with the mobs at Ephesus (1 Corinthians 15:32)? Were Paul and Silas "achieving fulfillment" when, beaten and thrown in irons, they sang hymns to God in prison (Acts 16:16-24)? Was Jesus trying to be fulfilled when He ministered to the sick and poor, or when he cried and died on a Roman cross?

Yet each of these people *was* fulfilled. Each had found the ministry and purpose to which God had called him. They may not always have *felt* fulfilled, in the sense that we often want to feel. Their fulfillment did not depend on feelings, but on the knowledge that they were walking within God's perfect will.

The men and women we now call "great" did not always feel fulfilled as they were accomplishing great deeds. The person who must always feel great will hardly ever become great. The person who must always feel fulfilled will seldom become fulfilled. God promises fullness of life. But we do not achieve it by striving after it. We receive it almost by accident as a result of pleasing Jesus (pursuing the Target). We don't get the prize by aiming at the prize, but by aiming at The Target—pleasing God.

Q3: Based on the people you have known, what are the characteristics of fullness of life as you picture it? As you list these characteristics, paint a picture in your mind of what a "fulfilled person" looks like. For example, does a life filled with activities cause one to be fulfilled?

The Self-perpetuating Machine

Apart from The Target—pleasing and serving Jesus—fulfillment is surprisingly elusive. We finish high school to earn the right to go to college, so that we may start a business or enter a profession, so that we can make a living and raise a family. We raise a family so that our kids can go to college. Then they can enter a business or profession to make a living and raise a family, so that their kids can go to school and earn a living and....

Yes, but what is it all *for?*

Life is a self-perpetuating machine. If there is nothing beyond the machine, then there is no purpose in life. "All is meaningless and a chasing after the wind" (Ecclesiastes 2:17). A dull routineness hits. We cast about desperately for something to make us come alive, but the answer cannot be found by searching deeper into the machine. It has to come from outside the machine. And the only source outside the machine is God, who sits enthroned in the timeless realm of spirits. He alone can show the way to fulfillment.

But one of the first things He asks is that we give up our right to be fulfilled. He wants us to quit trying so hard to be happy, and to seek to make Him happy instead. Not that He is so desperately unhappy that He must have us cheering Him up. But He wants us to know that He loves us, and He wants us to experience the fulfillment of a two-way love relationship.

Christ "died for all, that those who live should no longer live for themselves but for him who died for them and was raised again. (2 Corinthians 5:15). And here we are—back at The Target again! Living for God. "For whoever wants to save his life will lose it, but whoever loses his life for me and for the gospel will save it" (Mark 8:35).

It is only natural that we come to God with our private concerns, our little targets. We want Him to prosper our businesses, protect our families and guide us into a blissful retirement. We want God on our terms; we want Him to serve us.

But as soon as we give our lives to Jesus, parenthood, jobs, friendships, community activities, church work, school, marriage, relatives, money, leisure time—all become not so much ways for God to help us, but for us to serve God. As we give each of these areas of life to God, He blesses them, often in amazing ways. When He doesn't, we can still trust Him to know what is best for us. He wants us to seek first His kingdom and His righteousness (Matthew 6:33), and He will add deep joy, love and peace—the things that make life worth living.

Q4: Do you come to God with any particular expectations of what He should do for you? Where do these expectations come from?—TV programs, or the Bible, or denominational teaching, or personal longings, or a trusted friend or pastor?

Scripture Study for Chapter Five

- **Romans 6** (Walking in newness of life)

- **2 Corinthians 4:7-12** (The life of Jesus can be revealed in us)

- **2 Corinthians 5:15-21** (We live no longer for ourselves but for Christ)

- **John 10:1-18** (The promise of abundant life)

- **Matthew 16:24-26** (It is possible to gain the world; yet forfeit your life)

- **Luke 14:15-24** (Why some people do not want the Kingdom of Heaven or the Bread of Life.)

…And a little child will lead them.

6
Ultimate Hope

People are becoming pessimistic. A sense of foreboding is spreading out over the world. The threat of nuclear war, the horror of terrorist bombings, the curse of children killing children, the plague of false prophets who lead their followers to kill themselves, the growing fascination with evil and sexual perversion in our pop culture, the fierce persecution of Christians in many countries worldwide—the list of evils grows like multiple strains of bacteria.

Q1: Do you tend to be pessimistic or optimistic about the future of the world? Where do you gain your hope or your pessimism?

The Bible recognizes the evils that the world must pass through—the sort of thing that we have seen during the last two world wars. Jesus predicted that in the present age nations would try to conquer other nations, and war, death and famine would result— the "four horsemen of the apocalypse" (Revelation 6:1-8, Matthew 24:8). But He had a different point of view about these dire events than most of us do. We call them doom and gloom. Jesus called them *labor pangs*.

Labor Pangs

One day Jesus was walking by the gates of Jerusalem. He correctly predicted that the massive and impressive temple built by Herod would be cast down, and that Jerusalem would be destroyed (Matthew 24:1-3). His disciples, assuming that Jesus was prophesying His return at the end of the age, asked Him to identify the date and time of His return (when, it was assumed, He would reign on earth according to the promise of Zechariah 14).

He refused to tell them anything about this.

Instead, He said that they were not to assume He was going to come back during their life-time. He said that nation would rise up against nation, as Titus did in 70 A.D. to destroy Jerusalem. There would be wars, famines and earthquakes. These would be only the first of many similar events, all "labor pangs."

In times of unrest, people are eager to latch on to dynamic leaders who hold out promises. Jesus warned His followers that false prophets would come and try to lead many astray for their own purposes. At other times, people would actually claim to be the Christ. Jesus warned His disciples not to go after the false Christs and false prophets, but to stay close to Him. He would help them discern between the true and the false.

The rest of the Bible is equally clear about the suffering that must happen in this world, and the idea of labor pangs is consistent throughout all these prophecies:

> We know that the whole creation has been groaning as in the pains of childbirth right up to the present time. Not only so, but we ourselves, who have the firstfruits of the Spirit, groan inwardly as we wait eagerly for our adoption as sons, the redemption of our bodies. For in this hope we were saved (Romans 8:22-24).

The Bible does not tell us that life on earth is going to be easy, even for those who follow Jesus. Paul said, "We must go through many hardships to enter the kingdom of God" (Acts 14:22). But calling the sufferings of the world labor pangs implies a delivery and a birth to follow. God has a new creation ready to be birthed. This long-term promise gives hope in the midst of pain:

> A woman giving birth to a child has pain because her time has come; but when her baby is born she forgets the anguish because of her joy that a child is born into the world. (John 16:21)

Though God created this world, it has become separated from Him. Evil happens. But God is not willing to let history have a bad ending. He is going to send Jesus back to rescue Creation and return it to righteousness. This is another of the great promises of scripture, a future so different from the present that we can hardly imagine it. It gives hope to the despair we have when we look at depressing world events. God wants us to have hope and to speak hope.

Q2: Have you ever given birth to a baby or witnessed a birth? What do you imagine the Bible is telling us about the future when it compares history to a birth experience?

The Forgotten Promise

As a member of a mainline denominational church, I do not remember as a boy ever once hearing a sermon about—the return of Jesus Christ at the end of this age. Yet this promise has been a feature of basic Christianity from ancient times:

> And He shall come again with glory to judge both the living and the dead; whose kingdom shall have no end.[1]

I have often wondered: Why have so many Christians in our time (at least in the mainline churches) lost track of this basic promise? I believe it is because for so many years we went along with a false hope: that through scientific progress, we could usher in world peace and universal prosperity. All we needed to do was to build more schools and spread more scientific knowledge and technology. Educate! Educate! Educate!

Progress and Utopia

In the 1920's, Sigmund Freud, an atheist, expressed this hope:

> We believe that it is possible for scientific work to discover something about the reality of the world through which we can increase our power and according to which we can regulate our life.... Science has many open, and still more secret, enemies among those who cannot forgive it for having weakened religious belief and for threatening to overthrow it....[2]

Ah, those were the glory days, days of confidence in scientific progress. Like the builders of the Titanic, most people, at least in Western countries, thought that even God could not sink our ship. Freud, like many, believed that Christianity was an illusion, a house of cards that hard-headed science was soon to demolish.

Most people at the turn of the millennium have given up this hope in godless science. We realize that, whatever its "miracles" and achievements, it has given us just as many ways to destroy ourselves, as to achieve utopia.

I remember the stories about Reinhold Niebuhr, a theological professor in one of the denominational seminaries several decades ago. Niebuhr believed in the return of Jesus at the end of the age—believed in it at a time when such faith was not at all popular. He wrote:

> The man on the cross turned defeat into victory and prophesied the day when love would be triumphant in the world. But the triumph would have to come through the intervention of God. The moral resources of men would not be sufficient to guarantee it. A sentimental generation has destroyed this apocalyptic note in the vision of the Christ. It thinks the kingdom of God is around the corner, while he regarded it as impossible of realisation, except by God's grace.[3]

It is said that Niebuhr's students and fellow professors tried to talk him out of this particular part of his faith. They considered it ridiculous, a sort of archaic "pie in the sky bye and bye," a grasping after straws. It didn't fit the new worldview elicited by scientific progress. But Niebuhr believed the intervention of Christ at the end of the age was our only hope. He knew that utopia based on scientific progress is a futile hope. Surely subsequent history has proven Niebuhr right?

The New Age?

More recently we have the New Age movement—a faith in the power and teachings of spirit guides, propagated through countless occult societies and alternative religions. Dr. Carl Jung, the Swiss psychiatrist and guru of neo-Gnosticism, made this option popular at the end of the twentieth century. The result is a whole network of New Age bookstores and societies.

Curiously, most if not all of the instigators of the great conflicts and world wars of our time were following this hope, the New Age hope, when they grasped after power. For example, Alexander Dumas tells us that Napoleon, at the beginning of his soldierly career, visited the most famous psychic in Paris, a Mademoiselle Lenormand. Dumas has her telling Napoleon:

...You will be the glorious man, the man of prodigies and miracles. You will be Alexander, you will be Caesar, you will be even greater than they; you will be Atlas bearing the world.[4]

Needless to say, Napoleon did not achieve this dream. The powers behind him were only permitted to go so far with this promise. Then the promise was crushed. Many other world leaders have received similar words of promise from occult spirits, particularly Kaiser Wilhelm II and Adolph Hitler—as I have documented in *The Collapse of the Brass Heaven*[5].

A now-familiar pattern emerges from recent world history: A nation rejects God, as France rejected God during the French Revolution. Psychics and occult societies move in to fill the spiritual void. Occult spirits move through these individuals and societies to raise up a leader. This person becomes convinced that he is chosen to rule the world. Hitler, for example, believed that he was destined to establish a thousand-year Reich to rule the world—a counterfeit of the millennial reign of Jesus.

Every one of these world leaders ended his career bitterly disillusioned, recognizing that he had been deceived. The Bible tells us that all who try to rule the world will fail because only Jesus is the Anointed One of God—King of kings and Lord of lords.

Jesus Is the Christ

The biblical hope for a new creation here on earth is centered on the person of Jesus. Jesus is called "Christ." This is not His last name; it is His title. *Christ* means "anointed one." When we call Jesus *the Christ*, we are saying that He is God's choice to be king of the earth.

That is an exclusive claim. It excludes Satan and all pretenders to the throne of world domination, like Napoleon, Kaiser Wilhelm II, Joseph Stalin and Adolph Hitler, as well as a future world leader whom the Bible calls "the man of sin" (2 Thessalonians 2:3-4).

When Jesus called Himself *the Son of Man*, He was identifying Himself as the fulfillment of the prophecies of Daniel. This Jewish prophet prophesied a king who would crush all other kingdoms of the earth, and whose kingdom would last forever. During the Roman Empire, Jesus would ascend into the presence of God, where He would receive great kingly authority (Daniel 2:44, 7:13-24).

The Bible says that Jesus will return to the earth to defeat Satan, "the god of this world" (Zechariah 14:1-9, Matthew 24:26-31, 1 Thessalonians 4:13-18, Revelation 19:11-16). He will command His angels to destroy the Satanic host "at the last trumpet" (Revelation 11:15-19, Revelation 14:14-20). Christians who have died will be raised from the dead; those who are alive will be bodily lifted into the air away from the scene of God's wrath (Revelation 11:11-12, 1 Thessalonians 4:13-18). Satan and all who serve him will be destroyed "by the breath of his mouth," that is, by the Holy Spirit, who has far more power than evil spirits (2 Thessalonians 2:8).

After that, Jesus will reign supreme, bringing a new society, a creation that encompasses both heaven and earth (Revelation 21, 22, Isaiah 65:17-25). This will be a society of great peace, in which peoples' relationship with God and with each other will be as they were meant to be. Jesus, the true King by God's decree, will rule in everyone's hearts, having cast out all causes of sin.

God's plan for bringing peace on earth thus proceeds by stages:
- God provides a sacrifice for sin, by which people can be saved
- Jesus sends the Holy Spirit to prepare us for life with God
- Jesus comes back to destroy Satan and the hosts of evil
- God eventually creates a new heaven and a new earth

Q1: The power we put our confidence in at the present tends to be what we also put confidence in for the future. Among the three great sources of power—science, New Age spirits and God—which have you put your confidence in up until now?

Many people feel keenly the injustices and evils of this world, and they hunger after righteousness. Jesus promises that these, too, shall be satisfied with His bread (Matthew 5:6). That is why God intends to send Jesus back here. Jesus will bring the Kingdom of God, so that "His kingdom may come and His will be done on earth as it is in heaven" (Matthew 6:10).

Let's review the evidence of this ultimate promise about Jesus' return to earth—His "second coming."

Old Testament Promise

First, we have Old Testament prophecies like this one:

The wolf will live with the lamb,
the leopard will lie down with the goat,
the calf and the lion and the yearling together;
and a little child will lead them.
...They will neither harm nor destroy in all my holy mountain,
for the earth will be full of the knowledge of the Lord
as the waters cover the sea.
In that day the Root of Jesse [the "son of David," Jesus] will stand
as a banner for the peoples; the nations will rally to him and his place
of rest will be glorious. (Isaiah 11:6,9,10)

This type of peace may be hard to imagine. Yet we are encouraged to believe in it because of the number of prophecies about Jesus in the Old Testament that have already come true at his first coming. For example, the Old Testament correctly identified many of the details of Jesus' life:

- The place of His birth (Micah 5:2)
- The place He began His ministry (Isaiah 9:1-6)
- The purpose of His coming—an atoning sacrifice (Isaiah 53)
- The time He would first appear (Daniel 2:44, 9:20-27)

Like a string of dominoes, the first dominoes already fallen lead us to believe that the others will also fall. If half of the Old Testament Messianic prophecies have come true, we are encouraged to believe in the others as well. Their fulfillment is just a matter of time, though opinions may differ about how God will bring them to pass.

First-fruits of the Holy Spirit

Second, the apostle Paul spoke of "the first-fruits of the Holy Spirit." Christ has "given the earnest of the Spirit in our hearts" (2 Corinthians 1:22 KJV). The Greek word, *arrabon,* refers to the earnest money a prospective home-owner puts down on a house to guarantee its full purchase. In other words, the Holy Spirit, God's "earnest money," comes into our lives bringing the actual "money of the Kingdom." This is God's currency which we are privileged to trade back and forth until He comes again (Luke 19:11-13).

In short, the Holy Spirit brings faith, hope and love, in other words, the Kingdom of God, which will prevail during the future reign of Jesus Christ. This is another sort of evidence for the future kingdom of Jesus—the earnest money that the Holy Spirit puts into our spiritual bank accounts. More about this in the next chapter.

The Book of Revelation

Then, of course, there is the *Revelation,* the last book of the Bible. This extraordinary letter wraps up the entire Bible, drawing strands from hither and yon and tying them together so that we can glimpse how God's dealings with people will end.

This book is not written to strike fear in our hearts about the awful things that will happen at the end of the age. Like all biblical prophecy, the *Revelation* is written for our encouragement as Christians. The book consists of seven more or less distinct visions, each of which ends with good news.[6]

Like the rest of the New Testament, *Revelation* shows us that all tribulations are labor pains, and they are producing something incredibly good in the future. For example, in Revelation 5, we see Jesus, the Lamb of God, rising up into heaven during His ascension (which happened after His resurrection—Acts 1:1-11). Then He receives all authority in heaven and on earth. This authority is pictured as a scroll, which turns out to be the title deed to the world.[7]

In Bible times, deeds were scrolls sealed with a seal. You couldn't legally tear off the seal until you had paid the price of the property. Jesus paid the price to re-purchase the whole world for the Creator. During the present age, He is ripping off the seals on the scroll. Each seal is a form of suffering—war, famine, earthquakes, nations conquering nations, death, and so on. But we are to understand that these events are hastening the day of His coming. You see? The pains of tribulation are really labor pangs hastening a new birth. The disasters of this world are seals ripped off the scroll, leading to the full rulership of Christ.

This is how the Bible consistently pictures our future. It is a future full of hope, despite the seeming evils that abound. Christians should not set their eyes on the evils, but on the new creation that God has promised. Jesus is the "Alpha"—the first letter of the Greek alphabet. He began something—the kingdom of God, the purchase of the earth from sin and satanic domination. But Jesus is also the "Omega"—the last letter of the alphabet: He will finish what He began.

Q4: Does the basic idea that God wants history to have a good end change your basic view about the future? Could it have any effect on the way you live and work in the present time?

Scripture Study for Chapter Six

- **Matthew 24** (Jesus' end-time predictions)
- **Revelation 19** (The final triumph of Jesus the King)
- **1 Thessalonians 4:13-5:11** (Be comforted with this hope.)
- **2 Thessalonians 2** (All Christian ministry is rooted in the hopes Jesus gives us)
- **Romans 8:18-25** (Labor pangs are inevitable if the new creation is to be birthed)
- **1 Corinthians 15:35-58** (We are not laboring in vain)

He marks his maps with magic markers, and dreams of the places he reads about. But he never actually takes the trip he plans.

7

The Promise of the Holy Spirit

Like so many Americans raised during the fifties and sixties, I learned early in life to value material things, and to ignore spiritual things. Accumulating possessions was what excited people in those days. "The good life" meant having many of the things of this world—from swimming pools to big-screen TV's to three-car garages. It never occurred to most people to think of material things as "empty." Nor did it seem like much of a sacrifice when we neglected our children and spouses in the pursuit of such things. Material things, we thought, were what made people happy. You could not convince us otherwise because we knew we were right.

We were the Baby Boomer generation. Today, the Baby Buster generation is telling us what were the costs of this way of thinking. They have seen first-hand the emptiness of material pursuits because for them, material things have not created love. Many of the young today have grown up in homes where the investment of love was replaced with investments in stocks, salaries, retirement packages and corporate ladder-climbing.

God defines success differently: faith working through love. Jesus challenged a rich man to give his money to the poor and "Come, follow me." The man went away sorrowful, sensing that his money was too great an obstacle, preventing him from sincerely following Jesus.

The idea that material things could be a curse—which was Jesus' point of view—has not occurred to us Baby-Boomers until recently. We simply swept that part of God's message out of sight:

Do not store up for yourselves treasures on earth, where moth and rust destroy, and where thieves break in and steal. But store up for yourselves treasures in heaven, where moth and rust do not destroy, and where thieves do not break in and steal. For where your treasure is, there your heart will be also. (Matthew 6:19-21)

So we fix our eyes not on what is seen, but on what is unseen. For what is seen is temporary, but what is unseen is eternal. (2 Corinthians 4:18)

It is written: "Man shall not live on bread alone, but on every word that comes from the mouth of God. (Matthew 4:4)

Q1: Do you see any dangers in becoming focused on material possessions? Do you see other people falling into those dangers?

A Huge Appetite!

The materialistic version of Christianity that prevailed in the U.S. until the '70's left me with a gnawing spiritual hunger that I could not ignore. Worship, prayer and the promises of God—all were like dead leaves to me. There did not seem to be any food there, and most of us wanted to rake these things away as "irrelevant" to humans. Yet I went to church, as I had been taught to do, out of religious habit.

...Until, that is, I met Wilma Evey. "Willie" was a member of the first church I served after I was ordained into the ministry. Sensing my spiritual hunger, she came to my office one day to tell me about her encounter with the Holy Spirit—how she had asked Jesus to "baptize her with the Holy Spirit," and how something deep had happened to her after she had prayed that prayer.

I had never heard anyone talk like that. Nor had I heard anyone speak so fervently about Jesus—as though He were a real person who did real things for her. But what, more than anything, made me want to listen to her was this: Willie was the first person I had ever met who really seemed to *possess* the joy, love and peace of the Christian life. Others only seemed to talk about these things as intellectual truths in Sunday school class. Willie would sit in the same pew at the back of the church Sunday after Sunday and beam at me as though she knew a secret she was just bursting to tell me. And there she was that day, ready to tell it to me in my office.

Hold On. Wait a Minute!

Because her talk about the Holy Spirit was so new and different from anything I had learned as a believer in the gospel of American materialism, it took me about nine months of often soul-shaking searching to check it out. I could hardly believe that what she was saying about the Holy Spirit was true. I was a hard-headed intellectual and a cold-hearted Presbyterian all rolled into one. Fire and water (to which the Holy Spirit is often compared) were not likely to melt my skepticism overnight!

Yet God was beckoning to me through that spiritual hunger that I could not ignore. I read voraciously the scriptures about the Holy Spirit, and listened to tapes and testimonies of other people who had been awakened to the power of the Holy Spirit.

As I evaluated this "life in the Spirit," I uncovered a controversy brewing among Christians. Some books I read said that you "get" the Holy Spirit automatically when you become a believer in Jesus. Others said that you don't "get" the Holy Spirit until you subsequently speak in tongues. It was all so very confusing.

Experiencing God

In the end, I had to simply put this controversy on the shelf, ask God to show me what He wanted for me, and then move forward to receive whatever He gave. I was not so interested in solving doctrinal controversies, as feeding my spiritual hunger. I sensed that the Holy Spirit was the Giver of Experience, and that was what I so desperately needed: some kind of experience of God. My faith until then had been entirely too hypothetical and second-hand.

Some people were saying that we should distrust experiences of God, and that we shouldn't need them or look for them at all. We should just be content with following the Bible as a sort of rule book or a Giver of Dogma.

I admit, there is reason to be cautious when we venture into the things of the spirit realm. I have learned that Satan can counterfeit "experiences of God"—like he did with one man who heard "God" say that the stars in the sky were all spaceships and that he had been appointed to tell everyone about an impending invasion. I don't believe this was from God at all.

Because the spirit realm holds dangers, we have to test all things against the scriptures—or so I have learned since those early days. The Bible gives us the proper boundaries so that we can explore the spirit realm with safety. Because Jesus is the only one who ever came from the spirit realm (John 3:31-36), His teaching is the only reliable guide to lead us through it.

But to say that we should never go there at all, or that we shouldn't have any experience of the Holy Spirit, seemed to me rather like the person who plans a trip to a foreign country. He invests in maps and guides and Triple-A triptychs. He marks his maps with magic markers, and dreams of the places he reads about. But he never actually takes the trip he plans. For him, planning trips is preferable to making real journeys, because he can remain in the safety and comfort of his living room the whole time. There are no risks there.

I couldn't imagine that anyone would be interested in such a version of Christianity. I wanted to know God; I wanted to experience Him. If there was a being called the Holy Spirit who would come to me and make the Christian teachings I had learned in my church turn into Christian experience, then I wanted the Holy Spirit. If in Christ I have been raised up into "heavenly places" (Ephesians 2:6), I wanted to visit those heavenly places. I didn't want to only look at a picture of them in a tourist brochure.

During the charismatic movement of the '60's, people were testifying to their personal experience of the Holy Spirit. I was reading their books and hearing their taped testimonies. So I reasoned: Why can't I have an experience of the Holy Spirit? Does God love certain people more than others?

One verse of scripture leapt out at me more than the rest to give me assurance that I could actually experience the Holy Spirit:

> If you then, though you are evil, know how to give good gifts to your children, how much more will your Father in heaven give the Holy Spirit to those who ask him! (Luke 11:13)

Q2: Do you have any experience of the Holy Spirit that you could share with the group? What certainty do you have from scripture that your experience really was the Holy Spirit? Did it follow a scriptural pattern? Did it draw you to Jesus?

Four Ministries of the Holy Spirit

The Holy Spirit is a complex and many-faceted wonder. Let's look at His role in the lives of Christian people. These break down into four basic works.

1. The Washing of Rebirth (Regeneration)

The Holy Spirit has the task of taking the things of Jesus and making them come alive for us in each succeeding generation. When a person has this happen, he or she is said to be born again. God "saved us through the washing of rebirth and renewal by the Holy Spirit, whom he poured out on us generously through Jesus Christ our Savior..." (Titus 3:5,6). The Holy Spirit "takes what belongs to Jesus" and "gives it to us" (John 16:14).

Jesus' historical acts need to be applied to each of us individually, so we can appreciate how His life and death have changed our relationship with God. Many of us, for example, cannot believe God has forgiven us, nor do we have assurance of everlasting life. The Holy Spirit takes events 2000 years old and gives them to us with such freshness and power, it is as though they had happened this morning. He does this with all the things of Jesus. We enter into the experience of them as we open our lives to the Holy Spirit.

"I tell you the truth," Jesus said. "No one can enter the kingdom of God unless he is born of water and the Spirit" (John 3:5). God becomes real, Jesus emerges in His true majesty, the Holy Spirit becomes an inner "witness" that we have eternal life with Jesus (1 John 5:6-12).

2. Sanctification

The Holy Spirit has another job: to change us on the inside so that we become more like Jesus. "And we, who with unveiled faces all reflect the Lord's glory, are being transformed into his likeness with ever-increasing glory, which comes from the Lord, who is the

Spirit" (2 Corinthians 3:18). This process of inner transformation is called sanctification.

Here is a long-term promise, which, like the first one, deals with the inner person. Often, the most important, long-lasting miracles are hidden ones that God does inside us over a period of time:

- A harsh and bitter person becomes kind and gentle.
- A woman overcomes a lifetime addiction to soap operas.
- A man who is running away from his responsibilities at home starts to invest time in his wife and kids.
- A worry-wort learns to trust God with the problems of life.
- A businessman discovers beauty in the created world of nature.
- A teenager starts every day seeking God early in the morning.
- A devout racist begins to have compassion for people he has hated all his life.

These things have to do with the "fruit of the Spirit." We cannot expect that the character qualities of Jesus—love, joy, peace, patience, kindness, goodness, faithfulness, gentleness and self-control (Galatians 5:22-23)—will emerge overnight. But as we grow in Christ and ask God to change us, He sends us the Holy Spirit to urge us to make these inner changes—He cooperates with us in making them. The Holy Spirit awakens conscience, whispers new ideas about love, opens up true worship "in Spirit and in truth," and helps us walk out the pattern of sound teaching—faith working through love. More about this in Chapter Nineteen.

3. Empowerment in Ministry

Through a different set of promises, God also sends the Holy Spirit *upon* us, to clothe us with power. This is another dimension of the Holy Spirit, the "outer" working, as opposed to the "inner" working that we have seen above. Jesus promised that those who follow Him "will do what I have been doing. He will do even greater things than these, because I am going to the Father" (John 14:12).

When it came time for Jesus to send out His disciples as His witnesses into the world, He said, "But stay in the city until you have been clothed with power from on high" (Luke 24:48). In other words, Jesus did not want His people going out and trying to do God's work in their own strength and good intentions. He wanted us to be linked up with the Holy Spirit, and the Holy Spirit would equip us for whatever *God* wants us to do. More about this in Chapter Twenty-one.

4. The Fellowship of the Holy Spirit

There is something very unique that happens when people come together explicitly in Jesus name. It is as though Jesus Himself were there with them. This, of course, is what Jesus promised (Matthew 18:20).

Yet there is a problem: Jesus Himself is seated at the right hand of God the Father, and He is not coming back here until the end of the age. How then can He be "with us?" Jesus sent the Holy Spirit, who represents Him, and who brings His presence everywhere.

Wherever the Holy Spirit goes, people feel as though they are meeting with Jesus. There is no difference between the wishes, character and plans of the Holy Spirit, and those of Jesus—just as Jesus also perfectly reflects the wishes, character and plans of God the Father (John 14:9). There is no difference among them because they are all God. They are different dimensions or "persons" of God, each with His own function and responsibility.

Christians believe in a "triune" God—one God, but three ways that we have known Him—Father, Son and Holy Spirit. This concept of a "triune" God is difficult to understand, to say the least. One way is to make the comparison with H_2O, which has three different names, each for a different state of being—ice, water and steam. So, God, too, is known for His three different states of being—Father, Son and Holy Spirit. While this comparison may help our understanding, no image is really adequate to describe the mystery of the Trinity. This image, for example, does not portray the interpersonal love that exists between Father, Son and Holy Spirit.

At any rate, the fellowship of the Holy Spirit is a deep sense of kinship that rises up among people who are all seeking and finding Jesus Christ together. This is a kinship that goes deeper than having a common hobby, or a common complaint to talk about, or common ancestors. Having the discovery of the triune God in common with other people glues you together with them in a way that makes you true family.

Of course, not all Christians experience this wonderful fellowship. Like all the promises of the Holy Spirit, we receive them by faith. That is, we discover that God wants us to have this promise, we ask Him for it, we look for it, we do what He requires us to do to attain it, and soon the promise becomes ours. Nothing is automatic. Nothing is instant. Jesus calls us into a way that requires us to receive promises because we are hungry for them.

It is to this unique method of God—the walk of faith—that we now turn. If we do not understand this way of faith, then the likelihood is that many of the foods God offers us will remain on the shelf. So we must ask: How can we experience these things? How can we "eat" the promises and fully digest them, so they become part of us?

Q3: Of the above four ministries of the Holy Spirit, which do you believe that you have experienced? Which not? Is there any major area of promise that you feel is totally lacking from your life?

Q4: Pray for each other in the group, that God would supply what is lacking. If any group member has any hurts or negative experiences connected with the Holy Spirit, pray for the healing of those hurts.

Scripture Study for Chapter Seven

- **Titus 3:3-9** (The washing of rebirth in the Holy Spirit)
- **John 3:1-21** (Be born of water and the Holy Spirit.)
- **2 Corinthians 3:16-18** (The Holy Spirit wants to make us more like Jesus.)
- **John 14:11-14** (Because Jesus goes to the Father to send us the Holy Spirit, we can anticipate doing the same works Jesus did!)
- **John 16:5-15** (The Holy Spirit will be a reliable teacher in place of Jesus, taking the things of Jesus and giving them to us.)
- **2 Corinthians 13:11-14** (The fellowship of the Holy Spirit grows up in the Body of Christ, the Church.)

Do you open the door wide and let Him in? Or do you put the chain lock on, peek around the door jamb and mutter, "What do you want?"

8
How To Walk in Faith

We have been unpacking the most basic of God's promises in Jesus. Of course not every Christian has experienced all of these promises, as I hadn't during my growing up years. What so thrilled me as I entered into my personal walk with God back in 1972 was that each and every one of God's promises rested quietly in the Bible waiting to be discovered, unpacked, appropriated and owned. Sunday school truths that had been so unreal suddenly dawned on me in full digital color. God is real. His promises are real. His promises are for me.

Q1: As you look back at the last seven chapters, which of the seven basic promises listed there have you experienced to some degree, and which not?

   1. A valid purpose for living
   2. God's acceptance through an atoning sacrifice
   3. The knowledge of God, through an acquaintance with Jesus
   4. The rescuing power of God
   5. The zoe life of God welling up within
   6. The hope of Christ's return, annihilating despair
   7. The power of the Holy Spirit giving us what belongs to Jesus

Have you been content to sample only a few of these basic promises?

The Promises Come First

What I now saw was that I had very little to give to anyone else apart from receiving first what God wanted to offer me, out of the treasure-house of His promises. Sure, I had done well in school, excelling in many ways. But it all seemed so shallow and empty.

But then Jesus confronted me with these words:

> I am the vine, you are the branches. If a man remains in me and I in him, he will bear much fruit; apart from me you can do nothing. (John 15:5)

My attempts to "help" people had proven largely futile, but now God wanted to equip me with His gifts so that I could pass them along to others. This was a different approach to good works than the professional way I had learned in school.

Because I was geared to spend my life "helping people," the empowerment of the Holy Spirit for ministry caught my attention before any of the others. I realized that I needed the Holy Spirit if I was going to "help people." I needed not only the inner working but the outer gifts and manifestations of the Spirit. Our walk with God can start at any of the promises of God, and any of them can be the starting place to explore all the rest. Once you see that one of them is real, it is easier to believe in them all.

Apart from the promises of God, we are not truly discovering the way of Christ, but are likely to be practicing altruism—the religion of good works. This religion follows the love commandment all right, but there is no place for faith. It is an incomplete pattern. Christianity is more than good works, and it doesn't start with good works. It begins with faith in the promises of God.

True Faith Is Scary

"Faith," of course, means different things to different people. Some people think it means adherence to a set of doctrines. Others speak of faith as though it were a power in itself, and it didn't matter what you put your faith in. Faith healers, for example, believe that "faith"—not God—is what heals people.

To me, faith is more like letting Jesus into your life to do whatever He wants. Picture Jesus standing at your front door, knocking. You do not know who it is. You go to the door and open it. But do you open the door wide and let Him in? Or do you put the chain lock on, peek around the door jamb and mutter, "What do you want?" Do you even answer the door at all?

Letting Jesus in your front door is a step of faith. In the New Testament, one word, *pistis,* is used to refer to three ideas at once: faith, trust and belief. These three words, I discovered, can be used interchangeably. I have faith when I believe God; I believe God when I trust Him enough to do what He says.

To only recite the Apostles' Creed or affirm the existence of a supreme being somewhere in the universe is not true biblical faith. Early in my walk with God, God used Hebrews 11:6 to show me what faith is:

Without faith it is impossible to please God, because anyone who comes to him must believe that he exists and that he rewards those who earnestly seek him.

Those who have genuine Christian faith believe that when they allow Jesus into their personal lives, good things ("rewards") will happen, though they do not yet know what or how.

Letting Jesus come in can be a scary proposition because it means losing control, and letting someone into your life who could do anything. When I first let Him in the front door of my life, I was afraid of two things at once: that He would do something, and that He would do nothing.

I was stepping out into the unknown. This wasn't religion any more. This was God. I knew that God was bigger than I was. I also knew that God was uncontrollable. If God didn't do anything for me, then what would I conclude from that? That He didn't love me? That He isn't real? If God did do something for me, what if it was something I didn't want?

Is this the fear of the Lord? I asked myself. .

If He did come in and make His presence known, what would happen then, once He got inside? He might take away all my pleasures. He might cause problems in my family. He might ask me to do things I don't want to do. He might turn me into a fanatic. Or make me "religious" or completely loony! On the other hand, He might do what He promised: give me an adequate purpose, communicate His love, rescue me from my problems, give me ultimate hope, and the power of the Holy Spirit. Can I trust Him? Genuine faith is never easy. It is scary to let Jesus inside.

How God Encourages Faith

When my wife and I decided to give our lives and marriage to Jesus, God began to lead us into all kinds of experiences to build up our faith. We were ready to believe not only "that He exists" but "that He rewards those who seek Him." In a variety of ways, God began to show us how much He cares for us, if we will only trust Him more.

For example, my mother was stricken with a brain hemorrhage late in 1972. The diagnosis was confirmed by a spinal tap. My father, acting on his seed of faith, brought his concern to some Christian friends in a prayer group. As word of the brain hemorrhage spread, many people prayed for my mother that weekend. Members of a prayer group prayed with her in person and anointed her with oil. On Monday, symptoms of her illness began to disappear. An X-ray taken on Tuesday morning confirmed that the brain hemorrhage had been healed. That day she also discovered that a chronic back disability had been healed, as well as an ulcer, all in a day, the answer to prayer.

God does not always heal our sicknesses so dramatically or so quickly. I have often wondered: If He can do it in one case, why doesn't He do the same in every case of sickness, tragedy and pain?

I don't know the answer to that question. But I do know that God wanted to build up our faith, and that His healing touch for my mother encouraged her to step out in faith in other areas of her life. Faith requires us to step out, to pray and to accept God's word, even when we cannot be sure of the answers to all our questions. I have many other unanswered questions about God and the Bible, but I have decided not to allow them to hinder my walk of faith in God.

Q2: Most people have unanswered questions about God. Do you have any that consistently hinder your faith, and make it hard to trust God? List them. Do you have experiences that have led you to believe that God is not trustworthy? Ask yourself: "Why do these questions keep me from believing God's word? Can I put my trust in God anyway?" Bring these questions up during group meetings. Talk about these hindrances to faith, and try to get them resolved. Often, bringing them into the light will make them manageable.

Soon after my mother's healing, my wife and I both sensed (simultaneously, but separately) that God wanted us to give up a particular insurance policy, to spend the premium money for a Christian mission. The Lord does not usually ask us to give up insurance, but at that time, the leading was clearly confirmed, so we did it, trusting the Lord just a little bit more for our future welfare. We also began to tithe (give a tenth of our income back to the church), and then to move beyond a tithe in our giving.

These were scary steps. Yet we felt, with each step we took, that the Lord would care for us, if we would seek His Kingdom first. Based on the scriptures, His guidance, and the inner witness of the Holy Spirit, we believe the Lord was asking us to grow in belief-faith-trust. The point is not that insurance policies are bad (normally we believe in them), nor that everyone must give more than 10% of their income to the church, but that we are called to grow in faith and trust in God's promises, in whatever way God leads us.

The patriarch Abraham did it by picking up stakes and going off with his family to a far country, just because God asked him to.

> No distrust made him waver concerning the promise of God, but he grew strong in his faith as he gave glory to God, fully convinced that God was able to do what he had promised. (Romans 4:20-21)

This type of childlike faith is not widely accepted or even understood today, and I wonder if it ever has been. Jesus frequently chided the people: "What little faith you have."

Faith Is Guided by the Bible

To have faith is to reach out where the Bible tells you to reach out —and to your surprise, you touch something real! So you read the Bible some more, reach out some more, discover something more, and soon you are walking in faith. This is not blind faith, though the first few steps may be blind. In my experience, God does not often let us go far without giving us personal evidence that He is there, leading us onward. However, we must be willing to see the evidence! The Reformer, John Calvin, put it this way:

> Therefore we see that to us nothing is promised to be expected from the Lord, which we are not also bidden to ask of him in prayers. So true is it that we dig up by prayer the treasures that were pointed out by the Lord's gospel, and which our faith has gazed upon.[1]

When God led me to passages in the Bible that spoke right to me, I began to see His hand leading my Bible study. He teaches me! When He led two people to tell me the same thing on the same day, each without the knowledge of the other, I did not chalk that up to coincidence. I have come to agree with John Dye's view: "Coincidence is when God remains anonymous"—a quote from his mom.[2] More and more, I began to see that what I had once called "good luck" was not mere luck at all. I was seeing God behind the scenes, seeing with faith.

How does one begin such a journey of Christian faith-belief-trust? Look at Abraham. He ascertained what God wanted of him. Then he did it. He was demonstrating "the obedience that comes from faith" (Romans 1:5).

With us, too, the first step is to ascertain what God wants of us. We do this by reading the Bible, listening to God in prayer, talking to other Christians and becoming part of a vital Christian community where people are seeking God. Once we are convinced that God wants us to do something (like show love to a specific person, or forgive someone from the heart), we just do it, not because we hope to gain something by it, but because we believe that it pleases God. Faith that does not lead to some sort of action is not true faith (James 2:14-17).

The ABC's of Faith

In the scriptures there are hundreds of promises that God has given to believers. These promises will come true in our lives through obedient faith. Here is a simple ABCD process that I have found helpful in letting God's promises come true in my life:

A. Ask. Ask God to give you a particular promise that you find in the Bible, such as His promise of fatherly care in material things (Matthew 6:25-34).

B. Believe. Trust in that promise. Believe that it is true for you in your situation—that it applies to you.

C. Confess it. Whatever evidence God gives you, thank God verbally for it, as He brings His promises into your life. Thanksgiving can be a way of confessing your faith. A thankful heart (during an early morning prayer time, for example) can actually open your eyes to see God's answers when you might otherwise have overlooked them.

D. Do whatever God requires so that He can bring that promise true in your life (in this case, seeking first God's Kingdom and right living). Sometimes these commands of Jesus require wisdom, so it may be wise to get counsel from someone who is mature in faith. The promises come linked to God's commands. We can't have one without the other.

Faith Or Feelings?

Two other suggestions seem prudent to mention here. Prior to a walk of faith many of us make decisions on the basis of feelings. Even after we decide to try the Christian way, we measure the success of our faith-walk by our feelings. "Whatever feels good, do it" is a remarkably common guide.

But faith is an entirely different realm than feelings. God can give us some wonderful feelings. Love, joy and peace all touch us at a feeling level. But so do remorse, contrition and the fear of the Lord, which, though unpleasant, may also come from God. It may not feel good if others ridicule you for having faith in a God they have not yet learned to love.

My first suggestion, then, is: let go of feelings as your guide. Sooner or later we must all come off the mountain-top of good feelings.

Wait on the Lord

The other suggestion is to wait on the Lord to fulfill His plan. Most of us have become accustomed to achieving instant results. Many Christians expect to see lifetime habits disappear overnight. We want to see our spouses converted immediately. We try to make friends or fellow church members experience what we have experienced. We see problems all around us that we want taken care of by 5:00 today. But one of the most frequent commandments God gives to His followers is: Wait on the Lord (Psalms 25:5; 31:24; 130:5). There are two good reasons why God has to tell us to wait: the Lord is gentle, kind, patient and strong. We are not.

Q3: Have you ever been discouraged when the things you prayed for did not happen immediately? What was your response to this discouragement? Was it a valid response, as you look back on it?

Faith has been compared to a muscle which grows as it is used. Often, with the beginning steps in an experiment, the expectations are so great and the results so feeble that discouragement follows. To avoid early discouragement, begin with little steps, take them one at a time, and persevere.

Q4: In which areas of your life are you learning to walk in faith? Is there anything you are doing right now, just because you know God wants you to do it? Or is there any promise that God is inviting you to ask Him to give you? Try the ABCD process in that area.

Scripture Study for Chapter Eight

- **Genesis 12:1-7** (Abraham steps out in faith)

- **Romans 4:16-25** (So must we, in order to follow God)

- **Hebrews 11:1-12:2** (A definition of faith, with many examples)

- **1 Corinthians 1:18-2:5** (God saves those who believe. Faith in turn rests on the powerful acts of God)

- **Mark 11:20-25** (Faith will, in turn, call forth the power of God)

- **James 2:14-16** (True faith leads directly to obedience)

Once we have let Jesus in the front door, there are still many inner doors
to be opened to Him in our interior castle.

PART TWO

Responding to God's Wishes

9

Turning to God

God's word has two parts, and the two parts must come in proper order. First, there is the kerygma ("ker-IG-ma"), which is the proclamation of what God has done, and what He promises. Second, there is the didache ("DEE-da-kay"), or "teaching," which tells us how God hopes we will respond to His kerygma.

In the Christian life, *kerygma* always comes first. A relationship with God starts with God, not with us. His outreach to us comes before our outreach to Him. "You did not choose me, but I chose you," said Jesus (John 15:16)—and His words echo their truth into every generation. The first thing we have to do is to appreciate how God has reached out to us—and let Him reach *in!* That is the *kerygma.* Then we are ready to ask, "God, what do you want of me?"

Q1: Looking back on Part One (above), evaluate the ingredients of God's kerygma as they have entered your life. Has the proclamation of God's love strengthened or changed you in

some ways? For example, has it given you hope, joy, a new purpose, delight in God, a desire to worship, or a longing to know God better or to serve Him in some way?

Kerygma and Didache Go Together

In this next section we move into God's didache, or "teaching," in which God explains how He hopes we will respond to His promises. He invites us to learn what pleases Him.

> For you were once darkness, but now you are light in the Lord. Live as children of light (for the fruit of the light consists in all goodness, righteousness and truth) and find out what pleases the Lord. (Ephesians 5:8-10)

God's promises tend to take on an air of dreamy unreality until we have got both parts of His word working together in our lives—the *kerygma* and the *didache,* the promises and the commandments. "I will be your God" goes along with "You will be my people" (Ezekiel 11:20). It's a relationship, a covenant, an agreement between two parties. Aren't all relationships a two-way street? How can there be love, if only one person is committed to the relationship?

Though I have unpacked God's promises separately from His commandments, in practice the two cannot be separated. A person who tries to have the promises without the commandments, or vice versa, will end up having neither.

Jesus said, "Broad is the road that leads to destruction," and "Narrow the road that leads to life" (Matthew 7:13, 14). "Life" is a way. It is not just a set of beliefs. Jesus is not only "the Truth," but "the Way" and "the Life" (John 14:6). Belief in Jesus always leads to obedience to Jesus:

> Everyone who believes that Jesus is the Christ is born of God.... This is love for God: to obey his commands. And his commands are not burdensome...." (1 John 5:1-3)

First Steps

What are these commands? God's most basic longing is not complicated, but it may be surprising. Watchman Nee, the Chinese

Christian, put it this way: "We are *not* required—*in the first place*—to believe, or to repent, or to be conscious of sin, or even to know that Christ died. We are required only to approach the Lord with an honest heart."[1] He goes on to tell a story:

> I met a student once who said it was too early for him to come to the Lord. He wanted more time in which to taste the pleasures of sin and to enjoy himself. He said to me, "The thief on the cross was saved, but he had his fling, and it was high time that he repented. But I—I am young." "Well, what do you want to do?" I asked him. He replied, "I want to wait another forty years and have a good time, and then I will repent."
>
> So I said, "Let us pray." "Oh, I can't pray," he answered. "Yes, you can," I said. "You can tell the Lord all you have told me. He is the Friend of unrepentant sinners like you." "Oh, I couldn't say that to Him." "Why not? Whatever is in your heart, you tell it to Him. He will help you." Finally he prayed, and told the Lord that he did not want to repent and be saved, but that he knew he needed a Savior; and he just cried to Him for help. The Lord worked repentance in him and he got up a saved man.[2]

Remember the advice Madame Sheikh received as a Muslim woman who believed that God could not be known (in Chapter Five)? She was told to talk to Him as a friend or father—the same advice Watchman Nee gave to this student: an honest prayer.

Be Honest with God

Our response to God had best begin with honesty. God sees through all our little religious hypocrisies, our attempts to impress people and our false motives. When we try to build a life on top of untruth, everything turns out wrong. If the foundation is lies and self-deception, everything we build on it will eventually crumble. As C.S. Lewis wrote, "We must lay before Him what is in us, not what ought to be in us."[3]

Remember Harold Hughes, who prayed "the first honest prayer" he had ever prayed in his life (in Chapter Four)? One honest prayer like that is worth more than all the religious cover-ups in the world.

It is the one thing God is looking for from us. It is the raw material, without which He cannot build anything lasting in us.

God is the one person who knows us as we really are, and He loves us anyway. He is the only person with whom we can afford to be brutally honest and plain-spoken. If there is anything we learn about God from Jesus, it is that God cannot stand hypocrisy. Do you cringe when you are around people who are not honest? Do you rail against hypocrisy in all its terrible deceptiveness?

So does God. Jesus called such people "whitewashed tombs" (Matthew 23:13-22).

Friendship with God

But there is a point when each of us, religious or irreligious, church-goer or church-avoider, is invited to turn to God and begin a genuine friendship with Him. What good does it do to rail against "all the hypocrites in the churches" if we ourselves are not willing to pray an honest prayer? God has provided Jesus for us as the friend of sinners so that we will turn to Him openly and be vulnerable with Him, even if we have never been this way with anyone else. When we take this step, we begin to find the right course for our lives from then on.

Not that we immediately become perfect, or no longer have to struggle. Honesty with God is only the starting point, but it is the right starting point. We, at long last, are willing to have a friendship with God, and that is what Jesus came to give us—a friendship with God.

Q2: Do you have an honest friendship with God? Can you feel free to come to Him and speak forthrightly, asking Him for help, as the student in Watchman Nee's story did? Is there any reason why you think you cannot do this?

Is Friendship with God a Sacrifice?

In one sense, God offers His friendship to us free of cost. There is nothing you and I have to do (or can do) to earn it. But in another sense, His friendship is not free of cost. To receive and savor anyone's friendship requires us to spend time, energy and sometimes money to maintain the friendship.

Any time you spend money on something—a rare book or a sports car, or anything that you feel is more valuable than the money you spent for it—you don't call it a *sacrifice*. You call it an *investment*, or a *wise choice*. The only people who would call it a sacrifice are those who don't value the book or car as you do.

The same is true of knowing God. To those who want to know Him, the costs are not costly. They are simply the expected requirements of the most rewarding and satisfying relationship known to the human race. An investment. A wise choice.

The student in Watchman Nee's story thought that a relationship with God was not as worthwhile to him as pleasures he wanted to enjoy. But when he talked to God about those pleasures, God entered his life and became more real and worthwhile than the pleasures. God can do the same for any of us, if we will speak to Him with an honest heart.

Jesus' Greatest Parable

Jesus said that we should count the cost of being His disciple. At the beginning of His ministry, He was clear about what He expected of us. He said, "Repent and believe the good news" (Matthew 4:17).

This word, *repent*, is a common stumbling block. What was Jesus thinking, to use such a gauche and unacceptable word? Not only did Jesus start His ministry telling people to repent, but so did His apostles (Acts 2:38, Acts 26:20).

Jesus told a parable that, for many people, ranks as their all-time favorite (Luke 15:11-32). It is called "The Prodigal Son" parable. A man had two sons. Both were convinced that living with their dad was a pain in the neck. One of them decided that he would risk offending his dad, ask for his inheritance *before* his dad died, and move away from home. Amazingly, his dad didn't disinherit him out of sheer resentment, but granted the request. This younger boy then wasted his inheritance on wild living that left him a beggar feeding on pigs' food.

The boy then had a change of heart toward his dad. He didn't go crawling back to dear old dad to squander more money. Rather, his desperation caused him to wake up to the love of his dad, and to his own shoddy treatment of his father, which, he now saw, was totally undeserved.

He repented.

Notice this. In his repentance, he did not promise to turn away from any specific sin, except the way he had treated his dad. He saw that He had not valued life with dad, had wanted only to get as far away from him as possible. Now his eyes were opened, not because of any moral convictions, but because circumstances had caused him to appreciate his dad, and he wanted to be with him.

Jesus told this story to show true repentance. The Greek word *metanoia* means "a change of mind." That is what happened to the so-called "prodigal son." He changed his mind about his dad. He no longer wanted to run away. He wanted to come home.

False Ideas about Repentance

Sometimes we think that repentance means putting away every sin and living a devout and holy life. This, however, is not repentance but sanctification, which is often confused with repentance. Sanctification is a life-long process of change produced by the Holy Spirit in the life of a Christian, as I will describe in Chapter Nineteen. True, sometimes in our initial repentance, God compels us to renounce a specific sin (see Luke 3:8-14, for example), but that is not the heart of repentance. Simply turning toward God with an honest heart, and wanting a friendship with Him—that is repentance. Repentance is summed up in three words: "Turn to God."

Because many people have the wrong idea about repentance, it causes trouble in their relationship with God.

Some people say, "Just let me get my act together first. I have some terrible habits." They are trying to get rid of this or that sin so they can (one day, in the distant future) find their way into the good graces of God. They believe that God expects perfection, and it would be hypocritical to come to God while they are imperfect.

Others think, "I'm not God's type of person" so they cut themselves off from God entirely. Maybe they have a stereotyped idea about the kinds of people who become Christians (a certain race, class, lifestyle or "religious" bent.) Or maybe they believe they have committed "the unpardonable sin." But if they are earnestly seeking God, that cannot be true. The unpardonable sin is the sin of rejecting the Holy Spirit, who draws us to God and Jesus. Seekers-after-God cannot be committing that sin.

Others say indignantly, "God, look at all these things I did for You." They are like the elder brother in the parable. They dutifully stay put in the father's house, but resent every minute as though it were a prison sentence. They separate themselves from God while pretending not to.

Q3: Do you hold to any of these ideas, and if so, what effect have they had on your friendship with God?

Elder Brothers

Let's look at this elder brother in the parable. He hears a party going on and learns that his worthless brother has returned—and that his dad has accepted him back with joy. He cannot believe that his dad could have such a soft heart! Had he forgotten all the mean things the dumb kid had said to him?

I know Christians who remind me of this brother. They believe that Christianity is a set of religious duties that God requires of them. They think: *Why else should God exist, than to make our lives burdensome with religious duties, or to get people to go to church and to part with their money?* To them, every penny and every minute of their time is a "sacrifice" because their heart is cold toward God. They would much rather be buying things, watching TV, indulging in pornography, vacationing in the Bahamas or going after a reputation, yet there they are in church because they think God requires it. They cannot understand that all God is looking for is an honest friendship. They never give God the one thing He is looking for.

By the end of the parable, things become clearer. God patiently turns to the elder brother and says, "everything I have has been yours from the beginning." The elder brother could have enjoyed the father's love all along, but he was so busy doing his religious duties that he ended up as far away from the father as the "prodigal" son.

Q4: Have you ever been an "elder brother," or known anyone who fit the description? What does this additional part of the parable say about the cry of God's heart? Can you sense the cry of God's heart?

Jesus says, "Here I am! I stand at the door and knock. If anyone hears my voice and opens the door, I will come in and eat with him, and he with me" (Revelation 3:20). By turning to Him with a simple, honest prayer, it is as though we are opening a door and letting Him into the front hallway.

Of course, that is not the end of repentance, but only the beginning. Once we have let Jesus in the front door, there are still many inner doors to be opened to Him in our interior castle.

Scripture Study for Chapter Nine

- **1 John 5:1-5** (Those who believe in Jesus will follow His commands.)
- **Luke 15:11-32** (The prodigal son and the elder brother.)
- **Luke 18:9-14** (Repentant or religious?)
- **Matthew 4:12-17** (Jesus: "Repent!")
- **Acts 2:37-42** (Peter: "Repent!")
- **Acts 26:1-23** (Paul: "Repent!")

God made a table designed to keep us close to the cross.

10

Sacraments

Christianity is a relationship with God made possible by an atoning sacrifice. That is the bread. All else is sesame seeds sprinkled on top.

There are many counterfeit versions of Christianity around—and one thing they all have in common is that they do not invite us into a personal relationship with God—or He with us. They make Christianity seem like something other than what it is. They preach another gospel. One group claims to offer "the most perfect system of doctrines from the Bible." Another overwhelms us with religious rituals and secret handshakes. Another promises healing power and miracles, but not in the context of a relationship with God. These options offer the externals—doctrines, rituals, spiritual power and the like. But friendship with God is lacking from them, and that is what makes them counterfeit.

As we affirm every Christmas, Jesus is Immanuel—God with us (Matthew 1:23). Because of Jesus, we have access to God each day. Nothing can hinder that access, because it was bought with a price. *We* were bought with a price. Let us never allow ourselves to be talked out of what Jesus did for us. Jesus wants us to enjoy the benefits of His atonement every day for the rest of our lives.

To help us stay on track with God's intentions, God has given us the sacraments—baptism and the Lord's Supper. At least, most Christians call these sacraments (some call them ordinances), and the majority count just two of them.

"Be Baptized, Every One of You"

Back in the beginning of the church, God used the apostle Peter to give the very first *didache* to the first members of the first church, birthed on the day of Pentecost. As you might expect, Peter challenged them to repent, as we saw in the last chapter. Then he said, "...and be baptized every one of you in the name of the Lord Jesus Christ for the forgiveness of your sins" (Acts 2:38).

Bear in mind that Peter was addressing the very people who had just put Jesus to death, or who watched Him die and did nothing to prevent it. Through Peter, God was providing a way for them to get free from the guilt of their actions or inaction.

Likewise, God wants us to enter through a doorway called baptism. Baptism is the initiation into a way of life that knows and celebrates God's forgiveness. It is an invitation to respond to God's *kerygma*. This is one thing that virtually all Christians have in common down through the ages. They all believe that if you want to be a believer in Jesus, you should get baptized as a sign of that decision.

Baptism is our initiation into the way of Jesus as defined *by Jesus*. (See John 4:1-2 for John's description of how baptism got started as an initiation into Christ.)

Baptism shows us that Christianity is not just a head trip, a way of toying with various ideas about God. It is a way of life that has a beginning. It is all very well to read about the death of Jesus, as we did in Chapter Two, trying to understand it rationally. Ah, but each of us is challenged to *accept* it and then *respond* to it. Then, it will no longer be a mere head trip, but a way of life.

Baptism is not an altruistic deed. It doesn't feed any hungry people or do any practical good to anyone. A humanist would think of it as a worthless religious ritual. Its only value is that it comes from Jesus as a step into a way of life—friendship with God. Jesus does not want us thinking that we can get to Him by thinking.

"But I Think I'm a Decent Person"

There is something in us that wants to say, "I'm as good a person as the next guy. If anyone is going to be acceptable to God, I should be. I do my best to live right and my few flaws are minor ones. Why shouldn't I go to heaven?" To such a person, heaven seems like a human right, guaranteed by our Constitution to all people who are not felons.

People who think this way have never encountered God. They are speaking out of a terrible ignorance. They are putting their confidence in their own decency and comparing themselves with other people and judging themselves by their own culturally determined standards. Because they have never been humbled, they wear their own street clothes, as it were, into God's wedding banquet, whereas God wants them to put on a wedding garment that He gives them free of charge)Matthew 22:11-14). All they have to do is put it on. But instead of that they deceive themselves into believing that their own thoughts, self-evaluation, value system and abilities are what matter, and they refuse to hear the most simple instructions of Jesus and His apostles. While perhaps claiming to believe in Christ, they are not believing in Christ, or they would do the simple things Christ says to do.

Like get baptized.

In baptism, we are recognizing, in part, that it is not our right to dictate to God how we shall come to Him, or that He ought to save us if He knows what's good for Him. Instead, God has the right to tell us where our walk with Him will begin, and we must learn to listen to Him.

Q1: Do you believe that salvation and friendship with God are a human right? Or that God owes it to people to save them? Is there any biblical basis for that common conviction?

God's Answer to Shame

The Bible says that after Adam and Eve sinned, they "hid from the Lord God among the trees in the garden" (Genesis 3:8). To show that they were no longer willing to be vulnerable and open with God, they sewed together a contrivance of fig leaves to cover the shame of their nakedness. Ever since then, we people have felt the need to cover over our shame and our sin, and to hide from God.

This story pictures how God views the human condition. We have all developed elaborate psychological tricks for retaining some semblance of dignity for ourselves. We cover over our shameful deeds and thoughts with lying, self-defense, blame, rationalizing, drugs, alcohol, soap operas and many other addictions. We run away from facing up to what we have become in a fallen world. We justify ourselves. We investigate the trash in other peoples' lives so that we can say that we are not as bad as they are, or that they are just as bad as we. These methods are like clothing ourselves with fig leaves.

In baptism, God gives us another way of dealing with our shame and sin. Baptism is a way of taking the righteous act of Jesus and covering our shameful nakedness with it. We don't have to sew fig leaves any more, and we don't have to wear these street clothes. God provides a white garment. We can put it on. When we get baptized, we are declaring to all the world that we *are* putting it on. After that, we can remember, each day, that we have been baptized, and that we have put on Jesus Christ. There is no condemnation for us from God (Romans 8:1).

Q2: Have you ever been baptized? If not, what would prevent you from being baptized at the next opportunity? Or, if you have been baptized, reflect on what your baptism has meant to you. Did it give you a sense of being initiated into a way of life?

Inessential Variations

Getting baptized is a basic command. Beyond the basic command, it should probably be said that different denominations have developed various practices of baptism, no two alike. Some believe that baptism should be for believers only; others, that children of believers can be baptized also, based on the biblical practice of baptizing households (Acts 16:15,33; 1 Corinthians 7:14). Some believe in immersion baptism (based on the "burial" imagery of Romans 6:4); others in sprinkling (based on the Messianic prophecy in Ezekiel 36:25).

If you have already been baptized as a child of a believer, most Christians would say that you do not need to be re-baptized as an adult, though it is probably best to follow the practice of those who are nurturing you as a family of faith—your local church or Christian community.

Some people might say, "I was baptized as a child and it didn't mean anything to me." I have heard this just as much from people who only do "adult" baptisms, as from those who were baptized as infants. They feel that they were so immature when they were baptized that they would like to express their newfound deep faith and commitment to Christ by being baptized again.

However, the point is not so much whether it meant anything to you, as whether it meant something to God. God has given baptism as a sign of His grace and love, and the Church ministers it as such, even to children of believers (Acts 16:15, 33). There are no clear scriptural guidelines about age or maturity level except that the church is bound, whenever it baptizes anyone, to teach them to obey what Jesus commands (Matthew 28:19-20).

If you were baptized as an infant, ask Jesus to tell you whether you should get baptized as an adult believer. It is difficult to give a "one-size-fits-all" word of advice here, because today there are many counterfeit-Christian cults whose baptism Jesus may not recognize. At the same time, there is only one Church, with many denominational tags, and there is only one baptism (Ephesians 4:5). We should avoid quarrels about baptism, or thinking that every time we join a new denomination we have to get re-baptized (1 Corinthians 3:1-9). This would fall into the same trap as the Corinthian Christians, where some said that being baptized by Apollos was "better" than being baptized by Paul.

When we sense that God is ministering to our spirit, or that we are ready to rededicate ourselves to Him after a season of falling away, we should not get baptized a second time, or a third time, or a fourth. Baptism is only for first-timers. It is an *initiation* into Christ.

After that, we should come to the table that Christ has provided for all baptized believers—which is the other sacrament. The other sacrament, in fact, is an invitation to keep on renewing our relationship with God through Jesus.

Stay "in Christ Jesus"

Everyone has times when we feel far from God. Our faith and love are tested. We forget the important things. We become consumed with trivialities, absorbed in personal ambitions, or we relapse into self-reliance. We might even become alienated from God after we have enjoyed great miracles or a wonderful healing. It happens.

Maybe the evil one gets inside our brains and whispers what horrible people we are, and how we are not worthy to enter God's presence. Then we believe him. That was what happened to Peter on the night Jesus died—after having shared the last supper with his Master. Consumed with fear, he denied Jesus three times, and then wept bitterly about his own unfaithfulness. Jesus had predicted this, and had said that Satan was engineering this experience.

> Simon, Simon, Satan has asked to sift you as wheat. But I have prayed for you, Simon, that your faith may not fail. And when you have turned back, strengthen your brothers. (Luke 22:31)

Jesus knew about this failure before it happened and pinpointed its satanic origins, though Simon Peter was probably not aware of the spiritual power working on him at the moment it happened. Later, Jesus appeared to Peter at the Sea of Galilee, and broke bread with him. Jesus communicated His forgiveness, His acceptance and understanding, and reinstated Peter to apostolic ministry (John 21:10-19).

Peter was going through a drama for the benefit of all the rest of us. Jesus was showing all of us that we will likely fall away from God from time to time. These may be during testing or sifting times, when God is challenging us to grow up in areas of faith or love—and we stumble and fall, like Simon Peter did. But then Jesus invites us to come back to the table and break bread, and He will renew His relationship with us. That is why we have the sacrament of holy communion.

I have experienced this fallenness many times. Some people think that pastors are on some higher spiritual plane than other people, and never struggle with temptation. This is definitely an illusion. For example, I have an argument with my wife because she hurt my feelings; or I stumble onto an Internet site that I should have avoided; or I catch myself speaking curse words, a habit left over from earlier in my life; or I struggle unsuccessfully to forgive another Christian who has wounded me. There are even times when I feel that God has let me down, and I get mad at Him.

Such testing times are normal, but they do not need to alienate us permanently from God. Jesus wants us, during the test and the failure, to remember His atoning death. He wants to draw us back to friendship with God. Just because we stumbled doesn't mean we have to fall into the ditch and stay there the rest of our lives. God made a table designed to keep us close to the cross. We can get up and crawl to the table and begin again to follow Jesus.

Holy Communion

This second sacrament, then, is a way baptized people can keep close to Jesus even when we feel unworthy of God. Some traditions call this sacrament *holy communion*, others call it *the eucharist*.

• Those who call it *communion* emphasize the love and reconciliation (with God and with each other) that flow from the cross.

• Those who call it *the eucharist* emphasize the attitude of thanksgiving (the meaning of the word, *eucharist*) that we bring to the table. Jesus Himself gave thanks as He prophesied His own death (1 Corinthians 11:24). So can we, as we remember it.

Q3: Reflect on your experience of this sacrament, if you have ever received it. Did you think of it as a mere religious ritual, or did it have a deeper meaning? What meaning did it have?

The Healing Power of the Atonement

The prophet Isaiah wrote:

But he was pierced for our transgressions,
he was crushed for our iniquities;
the punishment that brought us peace was upon him,
and by his wounds we are healed. (Isaiah 53:5)

The sacrament of holy communion is also designed to remind us of the healing power of the atonement as God exposes deep wounds that need healing. The most important healing, of course, is in our relationship with God. After that, God wants to heal wounded attitudes about ourselves that come from the devaluing of others. The sacrament reminds us of the high value God places on us, and we can remember who we are *in Christ.*

Lastly, God's healing can enter our bodies and bring physical well-being. When we are healed in our relationship with God, our minds and bodies can feel the effects, too.

In short, this sacrament restores us repeatedly to fellowship with God. It also forces us to confront everything that hinders our relationship with God (1 Corinthians 11:28).

Q4: Have you ever known the Lord to heal any area of your life— body, mind, relationships, spirit? Are you willing to submit wounds to Him for healing? In group, share any experiences of God's healing that might be helpful to someone else. The next time you receive the sacrament, ask God to show you where you need His healing and invite Him into those areas.

If you are already a part of a denomination or tradition, seek out your pastor and find out what specific beliefs and practices have grown up in your church with regard to the sacraments. For example, some churches require the sacraments to be ministered only by the clergy, others do not. Some abide by certain forms in the sacraments. It is best to go along with the practices of your family of faith, while at the same time recognizing that other Christians may do it differently.

Scripture Study for Chapter Ten

- **Acts 2:38-41** (Basic apostolic teaching for beginners)
- **Matthew 22:1-14** ("Come to the table!")
- **Galatians 3:26-29** (Baptized into Christ; clothed with Christ)
- **Mark 14:12-26** (The Last Supper)
- **1 Corinthians 10:14-22** (Communion celebrates Christian unity.)
- **1 Corinthians 11:17-34** (Get right with other people.)

They do not suspect that a great treasure lies hidden underneath.

11
Unpacking Biblical Treasures

When we turn to God with an honest heart, God begins to speak to us. How God speaks into our spirit is a great mystery, but He does. In the process, He begins to open up the Bible in ways that are beyond understanding.

In seminary I studied the Bible, dabbled in Greek, learned Hebrew, and even taught Hebrew a little. My professors considered me a good student. Yet during all that time, God Himself was at a distance, and my studies amounted to mere class work.

How I "Discovered" the Bible

Two years later, in my hour of desperate hunger (described in Chapter One), I turned to God with an honest prayer, "Show me You're really there." Then something extraordinary happened to me. I began to see the scriptures of the Bible as I had never seen them before. Suddenly, it seemed to me that the Bible was the *truest* book I had ever read. It described the true nature of God, my true standing with God, my true helplessness without Jesus, my true need for the Holy Spirit. I gained such an appetite for the Bible that, during the next several years, I made the pages of my Bible greasy from page-turning. As I read the Bible, the Holy Spirit came into my life and rebuilt my worldview. I gained a new sense of God's calling, and a vision for myself that has remained fulfilling to this day.

And yet I do not understand how the Bible came to be so full of life and truth. I can only affirm what others celebrated when they wrote hymns about Jesus "breaking the bread of life" to us in His word. I know what the disciples experienced that day on the road to Emmaus. They said to each other, "Were not our hearts burning within us while he talked with us on the road and opened the Scriptures to us?" (Luke 24:32).

From the moment we pray our first honest prayer, life becomes a classroom, and we have both a teacher and a textbook to show us God's way.

Q1: Have you ever experienced this type of discovery—you are reading the Bible and suddenly the words seem to leap off the page; they take on deep truth and meaning? How do you account for this mystery, and have you found any clues that have helped you unpack the "bread for your spirit" in the Bible?

The English Bible

There was a time when Christians almost lost track of the Bible. But God would not let it remain lost. There are lessons in this story for us.

At the end of the Middle Ages, the clergy insisted that the only true Bible was the Latin Bible, and they, the clergy, were the only ones qualified to interpret it. By that time, however, the clergy were notoriously corrupt. Many were after money and power. As a result, the vision of what life could be like with Jesus was lost, because the source of that vision—the Bible—was kept hidden.

Along came John Wyclif, professor of New Testament at Oxford, England. Something happened to Wyclif as he read his New Testament in Latin. He noticed that the picture of the Church in the Bible bore no resemblance to the practice of the Church in his day. Jesus' original vision for the Church had changed little by little, so that nothing of the original vision remained. It seemed to Wyclif that the Church was full of money-grubbers and power-grabbers. Monasteries, which had been started to help people follow God, had succumbed to the corruption of wealth.

Wyclif began to preach and teach what the Bible said, and to translate the Bible into the language of the people so they could read it for themselves. He also recommended that the Church give back its money to the nobility, who had given it to the clergy to "purchase their salvation" for them. (The nobles loved Wyclif; the clergy hated him!) Wyclif also developed teams of people, called "poor priests," who went out to the cities, stood on street-corners and gave out hand-copied portions of the Bible in English. Wyclif was the first to translate parts of the Bible into English.

God's Vision Statement

The Lollard movement, as this spiritual awakening came to be known, was the precursor to the Protestant Reformation in the 16th century. In England Henry VIII proclaimed himself the head of the Church and tried to stamp out this enthusiasm for the Bible. He correctly saw that if the word of God were to have authority in peoples' lives, it would drain away the authority of the king.

The man who championed the cause of the English Bible at that time was William Tyndale, who began a translation of the full Bible into English from the original languages. This translation was completed while Tyndale was exiled in Germany. After it was finished, Tyndale was hunted down by Henry's soldiers and killed.

The English Bible has cost a great deal more than the pittance we pay for it at the book store. God raised up men and women who were willing to pay a heavy price because He wanted to keep our hearts burning with the true vision of His Kingdom. The Bible is God's vision statement. Get rid of the Bible, and you lose God's vision.

The first book printed on Johann Gutenberg's printing press was the Bible. By today, the Bible, translated into the languages of 98% of the world's population, is the biggest selling book in the world.

Q2: Were you aware that the English Bible has been purchased with the blood of many martyrs? Do you think that it was worth the price, and why do you think that people like Tyndale were willing to die for it?

The Holy Spirit, Our Teacher

Those Reformers suffered and died for the sake of two convictions that they would not compromise:

- God wants everyone to have His vision statement, to read it for themselves.

- We should avoid an unhealthy dependence on clergy to tell people what the Bible says, but rely instead on the Holy Spirit to be our teacher.

The Apostle John (one of the writers of the Bible) believed that every Christian could listen to the Holy Spirit to interpret scripture:

> As for you, the anointing you received from him remains in you, and you do not need anyone to teach you. But as his anointing teaches you about all things and as that anointing is real, not counterfeit—just as it has taught you, remain in him. (1 John 2:27)

In this letter, John was warning his people about false teaching (Gnosticism—paganism creeping into the church disguised as "a new version of Christianity"). This was a serious danger, yet John's answer was not to gain a tighter control by keeping the Bible out of the hands of "ignorant lay people." He believed that his people could ask every day for the teaching of the Holy Spirit. John, a pastor and teacher, believed that the Holy Spirit would guard them against false teaching by giving them the true.

Overcoming the Difficulties

Yet many people have a hard time when they open their Bibles. For them, leafing through the Bible is like walking through a wheat field. They do not suspect that a great treasure lies hidden underneath. When they open the Bible, they feel like they are reading from the original Wyclif Bible of 1388—

he that hath eris of herynge; here he.'

How can we dig up this treasure, open the treasure chest and unpack what's inside? Some suggestions:

1. Get an understandable Bible. Often, I find that when new believers say to me, "I think I have a Bible somewhere," the Bible they pull out of their closets is a King James Version. The difficulty with this version is that it is written in 17ᵗʰ century English. Why place that stumbling-block in front of yourself, if you are just beginning to get into the Bible? Many people believe that the King James

Bible is the only true Bible, and that all other Bibles are corruptions of "the original." But this is a little like the attitude of the clergy in Wyclif's time, who insisted that the only true Bible was the Latin Bible. Certainly, the King James Version has the weight of tradition behind it. It is also one of the most beautifully written translations. But if you want to understand what you are reading, get a newer translation. I recommend the New International Version (NIV). If you can afford it, get an NIV Study Bible. Also, flexible leather covers last a lot longer than hard covers do. And, by the way, feel free to personalize your Bible with your own insights. Don't be afraid to highlight passages or write notes in the margins.

2. Learn how to use a concordance. Study Bibles have a sort of index in the back called a concordance. If you have a subject in mind that you want to study, you can look up that word (for example, "prayer") in the concordance. You can also look up other similar words (like "pray" and "intercede"). Under each of these words will be a list of passages that include that word, with the scripture location for each. You can look up those scriptures and get a pretty good idea of what God's word says about that subject. Some concordances are more complete than others, of course, but the advantage of getting a study Bible is that the concordance in the back matches the translation you are using. If you purchase a concordance, be sure it matches your version of the Bible.

3. Learn how to use cross-references. Most study Bibles also have references in the columns near the text. To use these, locate the passage you are reading in the column of references. The other verses listed after that passage will lead you to other scriptures similar to the one you are reading. Between your concordance and the references, you can do a pretty thorough study of almost anything in the Bible. Of course, if you are wanting clues about the stock market, don't expect much information about that!

Q3: What Bible helps, if any, have you found helpful? In the group share your experiences with various kinds of Bibles and Bible helps. If there is time, let the group do some hands-on study, using concordances and references.

Attitudes and Expectations

We gain the most from any book if we want to get from it what it was written to give us. Many people are under the impression that the Bible was written to give them *how to's*—how to handle their money, how to date a girl, how to overcome marriage problems. We want practical help with everyday problems. It is true, this kind of information can be ferreted out of the Bible and it can be a blessing to us. But taken out of context of life with Jesus, this "how to do it" approach can be legalistic and discouraging.

Other people look to the Bible for *ammunition*. They are having an argument with someone over a point of doctrine, and they want to prove that they are right. True, the Bible is a "sword" (Ephesians 6:17), but it is not *our* sword, to hack away at other people with. It is the "sword of the Spirit" that cuts surgically into our lives to remove cancers and bring healing. The scriptures warn us to avoid "silly arguments" and "controversies" (2 Timothy 2:14, 23).

Other people are looking for *great literature, ancient history, or proof of some scientific theory*. Every five or six years, for example, I read about some new "quest for the historical Jesus"—where scholars have a new theory about what Jesus was really like, based on a new scientific approach. These people are using the Bible merely to gain a reputation for themselves and their new theory.

The Bible is given to show who God is, what God has done, and how we can walk with Him. *Kerygma* and *didache*. Look to the Bible for these things.

Readiness

The key to unlocking the Bible lies in our attitudes about the Bible and about God. To put it bluntly, many people are not receptive to the word of God because they don't think they need it. They are not hungry for it. They are willing to receive it only on their own terms, and they pick through it as though they were doing God a favor.

I read recently the account of the American bombing raid on Tokyo in 1942, our American retaliation for the bombing of Pearl Harbor. One crew from that raid crash-landed in Japanese-occupied China, and were interned and tortured for three years by the Japanese. Mysteriously these crew members were given Bibles during their imprisonment. The servicemen were so hungry for God that they feasted continually on the word of God in the Bible. It was the staff of life for them. Why? Because they were desperate for true bread, the "life" that only God could give. All else had been taken away.

One Christian writer tells us why we have such a difficult time hearing from God:

> Our lives have become absurd. In the word *absurd* we find the Latin word *surdus*, which means "deaf." A spiritual life requires discipline because we need to learn to listen to God, who constantly speaks but whom we seldom hear....
>
> Through a spiritual discipline we prevent the world from filling our lives to such an extent that there is no place left to listen.
>
> ...We need to set aside a time and a space to give him our undivided attention.[2]

Some Christians, especially in the east, have developed the practice of occasionally withdrawing to a lonely place for a few days, taking only their Bibles and a little food (a loaf of bread and tea). They leave behind computers, books, televisions, radios and friends. Their goal is to hear from God, to absorb His vision for their lives. Perhaps we could learn from these brothers and sisters in Christ. Perhaps we are too full of other food to have much interest in God's.

Information Or Formation?

In our culture we seem to be fascinated with information. Everyone is trying to get more of it, as though we were addicted to it. But this so-called "information revolution" sparked by the computer industry is doing few of us any real good. It leads very few people along the way that leads to life.

The key to *zoe* life is not information, but formation, as Richard Foster and James Bryan Smith said in their book, *Devotional Classics*. Foster, among others, has been helping people to rediscover the old way of reading the Bible, which was known as *lectio divina*— "divine reading":

This is a kind of reading in which the mind descends into the heart, and both are drawn into the love and goodness of God. We are doing more than reading words; we are seeking "the Word exposed in the words...." We are endeavoring to go beyond information to formation—to being formed and molded by what we read. We are listening with the heart....[3]

This is the key to unlocking the treasures of the Bible—a receptive heart that is willing to be formed and shaped by the Holy Spirit. We come to the Bible with no pre-conceived ideas of what we should find there. God's thoughts are higher than ours, and so we are poor judges of what God should tell us. We simply ask the Holy Spirit to lead us to a higher level in our appreciation of God. We come to the Bible like little children, expecting Him to speak to us, as many other generations before us have found Him willing to do. Why not begin your Bible study by asking the Holy Spirit to use God's word to shape your future.

Q4: Looking back on the last year, think of some times when you got your Bible out and read it. What were your motives?—to be formed or informed? Are your motives for reading the Bible changing, as the Holy Spirit works in your heart?

Scripture Study for Chapter Eleven
- **Galatians 1:11-24** (Apostolic teachings are not of human origin, but are divine revelation.)

- **Ephesians 3:1-13** (These teachings are given to the Church to spread throughout the world, even into the spirit world.)

- **2 Timothy 3:1-13** (The scriptures are inspired by the Holy Spirit for our formation in Christ.)

- **Deuteronomy 6: 1-9** (Surround yourself with them.)

- **John 15:1-11** (Staying close to Jesus, let His words dwell in you always.)

- **John 5:36-40** (The purpose of the Bible: to draw us to Jesus.)

There are at least three types of prayer reported by Christians.

12

True Prayer

I have said that the beginning of a walk with God is an honest prayer. Honest prayer happens because God made provision for it. He sent Jesus. If Jesus had not done what He did, there could be no intimate communication with God. Apart from Jesus, prayer would be what it is among the non-Christian religions:

- A recitation of memorized words directed toward God.
- Requests made to spirits other than God.

Jesus Is the Door to God

In the darkness of the temple at Jerusalem there hung a huge curtain, a double layer of heavy cloth thirty feet square, occupying one whole wall of the Holy Place. It separated the Holy Place from the Holy of Holies, where God manifested His presence. It represented a fixed barrier that separated God from us. At the hour Jesus died, this curtain was torn from top to bottom as a sign that something significant happened to the barrier between ourselves and God (Matthew 27:51; Hebrews 10:20).

To those of us who are not Jews by birth, the torn curtain symbolizes a new access to God we never could have enjoyed without the death of Jesus. Prior to that event, we were strangers to the covenants of promise and without God in the world (Ephesians 2:12). But when Jesus died, the temple curtain was replaced by an open door. Jesus became "the door for the sheep" (John 10:7), that we might have fellowship with the Father, and with His Son (1 John 1:3).

"Daddy!"

When Jesus came among us, He called God what no one else had called Him: "Father." The word He used was even more intimate than that: Abba, "Daddy" (John 17:1, Matthew 26:39). He then taught His disciples to address God the same way: "Our Father in heaven, hallowed be your name" (Matthew 6:9).

Later, He gave His disciples the Holy Spirit (also called "the Spirit of sonship"), which would enable His followers to be adopted into God's household. Because of the ministry of the Son and the Holy Spirit, we can relate to God intimately as our Father.

> For you did not receive a spirit that makes you a slave again to fear, but you received the Spirit of sonship. And by him we cry, 'Abba, Father.' The Spirit himself testifies with our spirit that we are God's children. (Romans 8:15-16)

Christian prayer grows out of this intimate relationship with God that Jesus opened up for us. Yet many Christians do not think of prayer as intimate conversation. Prayer has been many other things:

- I used to think of it as a form of poetry.
- Others use children's rhymes taught by their parents.
- Others see prayer as meditation, to release them from stress.
- Others see it as a religious duty or a set of rituals God requires.

Q1: What was your experience of prayer in your early years and how has that affected your present prayer life? Do you sense that you have a daily relationship with God?

Whatever your background with prayer, prayer can become intimate conversation with the heavenly Father, as it was for Jesus.

I have been in many Bread groups where people took their first steps into this kind of intimate prayer—and discovered how God honored their first experiments in Christian prayer. People who had never talked with God began to sense that God was ready to listen and reply as a Father who loves them. Many people from non-Western countries have had this sort of communication with other spirits, but not with God Himself. Through Jesus alone, we can converse this way with God.

As we enter into intimacy with God, we soon find that there are at least three types of prayer that have been reported by Christians through the ages.[1]

1. Listening Prayer

The longer we walk with God, the more we realize that He wants to initiate His plans with us. He is like a loving daddy who says, "Come, won't you join me in a project I have in mind." The most rewarding enterprises come to us when we are listening to God, and God initiates a project with us. Of course, this requires us to sit still, clear away distractions, and make some quality time for God.

Soon we discover, as I did, that "We are...created in Christ Jesus to do good works, which God prepared in advance for us to do" (Ephesians 2:10). It is usually through listening prayer that we discover what these good works are.

Jesus Himself modeled out this pattern. Even when He was being sought out by great crowds of people, He always took quality time with God, going off by Himself to listen to the Father's instructions (Mark 1:35, 6:46). When frenzied people would come to Him saying, "You gotta come back. Everyone's looking for you," Jesus never allowed Himself to become a slave of their desires. Because He listened to the Father and knew the Father's vision for His life, He could do what He knew God wanted in each situation.

Jesus behaved this way as a model for us. He wanted us to learn how to get God's vision by listening to God.

Of course, we live in a more complex age than Jesus did. We have surrounded ourselves with TV sets, computer monitors, video screens and a Hollywood film culture, all pumping out vision. Most of us get our vision of what we can become from these instruments of vision, rather than from God. We all need a vision, for without a vision, we "perish," as the Bible says (Proverbs 29:18). Life becomes so humdrum that we can hardly stand the boredom.

But most of us have forgotten how to get our vision the proper way—by listening to God. Therefore, we at the turn of the millennium have provided for ourselves other ways to pursue our vision quest: TV, computers and the movies.

As we learn to follow Jesus, we can push aside the instruments of vision in our culture and listen to God instead. We can do this in two ways:

- by taking a part of each day for quality time with God—a "quiet time" suited to our schedules.
- by taking occasional retreats away from TV sets, computers, telephones, stresses and interruptions, to listen to God.

If we do not take time to specifically hear the voice of God, it seems unlikely that we will hear from Him. If even Jesus had to push aside the voices of an idolatrous culture to hear from God, is it not likely that we will have to do the same?

Some people wonder what it is like to hear from God. I used to be suspicious about this myself, especially when a few people were always saying, "God told me this" or, "God said that." I was not sure that God really had been speaking to them. Still, the Bible makes it clear that we can expect God to speak into our lives (John 10:1-5). What is it like when this happens? These are the ways God speaks to me:

- A scripture verse leaps into my mind with new and forceful meaning. "This is for you," God says.
- A powerful idea inserts itself into my mind, confirmed in scripture, in circumstances or by other Christians.
- A peace fills my heart, replacing jangled nerves, worry, fear or confusion.
- A dream, vision or picture pops into my mind, which applies biblical truth in a particular way.

Q2: Have you ever sensed that God was speaking to you? Jot down the circumstances and share with the group. See if you can come up with some principles about listening to God, based on the group's experiences of hearing from Him.

2. Prayers of Asking

Can you imagine a child who never asked her parents for anything? Surely such a child would be abnormal, and such a household would be unusually loveless. In this picture, fear or hopelessness or bitterness has replaced the normal freedom of the child to come to the parents with her requests. A normal, healthy relationship between parent and child includes the freedom to make requests. This is part of what it means to be a child of a father or mother. Not that the loving parent must always give what the child asks. But the child knows that her requests are welcome.

As the child grows older, the nature of the requests change. They become more mature—more in line with the wiser judgments of the parents. The child has begun to realize that the parents know more than she does, so she adjusts her requests to what she knows they want to give her. She is learning to ask according to their will. The freedom to ask them for things is maturing. But at no time does she outgrow her right to ask her mom and dad for things that please her. Because they love her, their door is open.

Which of you, if his son asks for bread, will give him a stone? Or if he asks for a fish, will give him a snake? If you, then, though you are evil, know how to give good gifts to your children, how much more will your Father in heaven give good gifts to those who ask him! (Matthew 7:10-11)

Many people believe that it is selfish to ask God for anything. But if we measure our understanding of God by scripture, we realize that this is a mistaken impression. Even Jesus asked God for things. He was a son coming to a father, and He did what was appropriate for sons with their fathers.

Accordingly, the mature believer is not a person who never asks God for anything. We would suspect such a person of being self-reliant, not God-reliant. The mature believer is one who asks for things that are more and more in line with God's will, not one who stops asking God for anything.

How wonderful it was when I first discovered that God was ready to call me to prayer, and answer my prayers. I remember one time when I was so troubled that I prayed and fasted for three days on behalf of my congregation. This was the first time I ever tried fasting with my prayer. I told no one about this. Yet, the day after my fast, a member of my congregation, with her husband, showed up unexpectedly on my doorstep. She said she had a word from the Lord for me, and her husband was making her come and give it to me!

I had learned to be skeptical about such claims. But it was apparent that this was a genuine word from the Lord, for it started out, "My son, I have heard your prayers." What an encouragement that was! Each point that she made was a direct answer to what I had been praying to God about. And during the following year, everything the woman prophesied did take place.

"But When *I* Pray, Nothing Happens!"

Some people never ask God for anything because they tried it once, and nothing happened. There are several possible reasons for this:

- They were not Christians at the time, and did not know that the door through which we approach God is Jesus (Hebrews 4:14-16, 10:19-23).
- They did not recognize the need for perseverance in asking. God has provided prayer as a way to bring forth His plans. But often this process takes time, like the conception and birth of a child. If we grow discouraged and stop praying, the thing does not get birthed. Jesus tells us to persevere (Luke 18:1-8).
- They were praying for something for which there is no basis in scripture, something that is opposed to God's will (1 John 5:14). God said "No," or "Later."
- Something was hindering their prayer and their relationship with God. Prayer power seems to grow as we grow to maturity in Christ. Bitterness (Mark 11:25), pride (Luke 18:10-14) and dishonoring of spouses (1 Peter 3:7) are among the things that hinder prayer. In general, the power of prayer is related to the life of the person praying. Godliness and prayer grow up to maturity together (James 5:16).

Q3: Have you ever had an experience of clearly answered prayer? Jot down the circumstances and share with the group. Is it a worthy goal to learn to pray according to God's will?

3. Praying in One Accord

There comes a time in our prayer life when God shows us that the prayers of several people can have greater power than the prayers of one. For this reason, He wants to develop churches that become houses of prayer (Matthew 21:13). It is likely that He wants our homes to be houses of prayer, too (1 Corinthians 7:5). These ideas, which take us beyond simple private prayer, will challenge us to learn how to pray out loud with other people, and eventually, to gain the skill of "agreeing in prayer."

> Again, I tell you that if two of you on earth agree about anything you ask for, it will be done for you by my Father in heaven. For where two or three come together in my name, there am I with them. (Matthew 18:19-20)

In a Bread group, we can learn how to do this. Most people, at the beginning of their prayer life, are reluctant to pray out loud in the presence of other people. Prayer is unfamiliar and many people are embarrassed to reveal how clumsy they feel whenever they pray. It feels a little like the time I first tried to speak French to French people. I felt acutely self-conscious and inept. To many people, prayer is a foreign language. Perhaps they do not realize they can talk to God in the same ordinary words they use when talking to anyone else.

When it comes to learning how to agree in prayer, I suggest that a group start a little experiment. When someone prays for a particular concern—for example, a job interview—then before the group moves on to pray for something else, at least one other person in the group should also pray for that job interview. So, the group learns how to agree in prayer.

Sometimes, group prayer feels a little scattered. One person prays for their uncle Joe to be healed, another prays for the President of the United States, another confesses a sin that has been weighing on him, and then someone else starts to sing a praise song. It seems as though everyone is praying in their own little world. There is no focus, and the prayer is getting nowhere.

When this happens, I recommend that a group follow a pattern in prayer that will help to move the group together in a journey. The journey has a beginning, a middle and an end, and everyone is moving on the same journey. The stages of the journey (which can also guide private prayer) are these:

- Adoration (We tell God our appreciation of Him.)
- Thanksgiving (We remember the things God has done.)
- Confession of sin (We tell Him our failures, asking help for the future.)
- Petitions (We present our needs.)
- Intercessions (We finish with our concerns for others.)

In a group, sometimes it helps for the leader to actively lead prayer by saying, "Why don't we start with a little praise." That helps the whole group to be more unified as the leader moves the group from stage to stage in the prayer journey.

Q4: How do you feel about praying out loud with other people, who are learning to agree in prayer? If you have objections to this, list them, and ask yourself where these objections come from.

Scripture Study for Chapter Twelve

- **Mark 1:35-39** (Jesus prays.)
- **Matthew 26:36-46** (Jesus struggles in prayer.)
- **Matthew 6:5-13** (Jesus rebukes false prayer—not public prayer.)
- **Luke 18:1-8** (Persevering in prayer)
- **Matthew 18:19-20** (Agreeing in prayer with other believers)
- **Romans 8:12-27** (The Holy Spirit helps us pray by linking us intimately with the Father.)

In the Bible, worship almost always included some form of sacrifice.

13

Worship and Praise

We are ready to put the two halves of the pattern of Christ together—faith and love. These are separable only for the sake of discussion. In practice, they have a symbiotic relationship: without each other they each sicken.

The only thing that counts is faith expressing itself through love. (Galatians 5:6)

Here is the pattern of sound teaching that is unique to Jesus and the Bible, the pattern that God wants to produce in all of us. Not faith only, but faith working through love, faith flowing into love, faith expressing itself in love. If we have this foundation, we can build much on top of it. If not, whatever we build is likely to collapse. When we find the way to live out this pattern from day to day, it is surprising how much better everything goes. It is the way that leads to life.

What you have heard from me, keep as the pattern of sound teaching, with faith and love in Christ Jesus. (2 Timothy 1:13)

Love of God Translates Into Praise

I described how to walk by *faith* in Chapter Eight. But what is *love*, and how do we do it? This question is not as easy to answer as it may seem.

Here is a husband who says he loves his wife, yet he never praises her, appreciates her, speaks of her qualities in anything but a sarcastic way, or shows that he values her. Can it really be said that he loves her? Only if we drain the word "love" of all its meaning.

The same is true toward God. Praise gives love its shape.

I once entered a contest to memorize the Westminster Confession of Faith. My "human computer" failed to include a few lines here and there, so I didn't win the contest. But one idea from that Confession of Faith did sink in: "The chief end of man is to glorify God and enjoy Him forever."

It was not until three years later, when I came to Jesus and began to rely on His promises, that glorifying God became a desire of my heart. The Holy Spirit filled me with appreciation for all God had done in Jesus. I entered a honeymoon with God. And during this honeymoon worship emerged, not so much as a religious duty, but as the expression of genuine love for Him. I had come into an intimate friendship with God, and I had to find ways to express it in plain and sincere language. I gained a new appreciation for the classic hymns of the church, and learned all kinds of new praise songs, as well. I kept looking for more fresh ways of expressing love for God, because my love kept growing, and would not be contained in the old, narrow confinements. That which is fresh and new each day looks for fresh and new ways of expression.

After a year or two, the daily routine started to infiltrate this honeymoon love. Soon I found my praise-love of God being evaporated by committee meetings, TV watching and family vacations. God had let me see a glimpse of an alternative: truly living for Him, and not just pretending to. Then He let me have my natural life pattern back, and asked me to exert my will in whatever direction I thought best: toward Him or toward all the countless other things I had learned to "love." Not wanting to lose my new-found life of worship, I began to exercise my will. Though I had never been one to express love, praise, or appreciation toward anyone, I began to do so more freely now.

Worship Is Showing Worth

To many people, worship is what you do at a Sunday worship service. But to me it is more. The word "worship" comes from the Anglo-Saxon word *wyrthscipe*, that is, "worth-ship." You worship

God whenever you are showing that He is precious—worth a great deal to you. When you can say to God, "I like you just because you're you," you are in a position to worship. But if you do not feel that way about God, you are not in a position to worship Him. No matter how many hymns you may sing, they do not add up to worship. The apostle Paul had arrived at worship when he said:

> I count everything as loss because of the surpassing worth of knowing Christ Jesus my Lord. For his sake I have suffered the loss of all things and count them as refuse, in order that I may gain Christ.... (Philippians 3:8, RSV)

In the Bible, worship almost always included some form of sacrifice (as Webster defines it, "a giving up, destroying, permitting injury to or forgoing some valued thing for the sake of something of greater value"). The way the Hebrews showed the greater worth of God was by sacrificing an animal or two which were valuable to them. They showed they loved God more than the things God gave them. They worshipped the Creator, not the creation; the Giver, not the gift.

But after a while, their sacrifices became a way of buttering God up so they could live shabby, self-centered lives without a twinge of conscience. The sacrifice became a bribe. God responded: "Though you offer me your burnt offerings and meat offerings, I will not accept them" (Amos 5:22).

By New Testament times God revealed what He had wanted all along: ourselves. "Offer your bodies as a living sacrifice, holy and pleasing to God—which is your spiritual worship" (Romans 12:1). God still asks us to show God's worth by a sacrifice, but now it is the sacrifice of our lives. Every time we give up doing one thing, and do something different because we know it pleases God, that is worship—showing God's worth.

Q1: Have you ever done something or given up something purely because you knew it would delight God, with no other conscious motives mixed in? What was the result? How did you feel about that act of worship?

Praise, a Form of Worship

I find it hard to stick to this "living for God," this "worshipping God with my life." How easy it is to get side-tracked, to become absorbed in some completely self-centered passion or pursuit. But God has given me a discipline called praise to help me: "Through Jesus, let us continually offer up a sacrifice of praise to God, that is, the fruit of lips that acknowledge his name" (Hebrews 13:15). Praise is worship with the lips. Worship is a way of life. Praise is worship in words.

Praise can prepare us to offer our bodies as a living sacrifice. The rest of the body follows along when the tongue leads the way.

Praise is sometimes a sacrifice in itself. Did you ever try praising God when things were not going your way? Your ham and eggs were too salty this morning, the neighbor's dog barked all night long, or your car wouldn't start? I once knew a man who praised God while he was digging out his septic tank. This was so unusual that it opened up a conversation with his neighbor about God.

Or maybe your problems are more serious: your company downsized you; you had a blowup with your spouse; you are stricken with a serious illness; or you totaled your new Lexus. Did you ever try saying, "The Lord gives; the Lord takes away. Blessed be the name of the Lord"? I am serious! Look at the prophet Habakkuk, who wrote:

> Even though the fig trees are all destroyed, and there is neither blossom left nor fruit, and though the olive crops all fail, and the fields lie barren; even if the flocks die in the fields and the cattle barns are empty, yet I will rejoice in the Lord; I will be happy in the God of my salvation. (Habakkuk 3:17-18, Living Bible)

If we love God only when we are prospering, maybe our professed love for God is only a hidden form of self-love. But when we love God just because He is God, we will tell Him so no matter what the circumstances.

According to Romans 8:28, if we love God and are called according to His Target, we can be confident that He will turn even the worst tragedy into good. The question is: when and how will He do it? But even before we know the answer to this question, we can genuinely praise God in the midst of pain and deprivation. We do not exactly praise God *for* the suffering, as though we enjoyed suffering. Nor do we praise God *despite* the suffering ("Praise the Lord anyway"). We praise Him in faith that He is going to use that very suffering or deprivation for good in His bigger plan. We may not see this bigger plan yet, but we can have confidence that He is working it out, and that it will reflect God's love.

God is in the midst of suffering. He has compassion for us, the sufferers. He has already achieved a victory, and promised a future without suffering (Revelation 21:4). If we are faithful He will eventually work out the details of this victory in our lives. Therefore, we can praise God in advance. As Paul wrote:

Be filled with the Spirit, addressing one another in psalms and hymns and spiritual songs, singing and making melody to the Lord with all your heart, always and for everything giving thanks in the name of our Lord Jesus Christ to God the Father. (Ephesians 5:18-20)

Praise Has Power

When we do this, it isn't just good for God. It is good for us. One summer, Carla and I took a vacation to visit our families. We were driving a Toyota, which didn't have air conditioning. If you have ever driven 600 miles for 12 hours, with two small kids in the car, you know what we felt like by about five in the afternoon. It was hot; the kids were cranky; my wife was tired of hassling them; and various parts of my anatomy were drawing attention to themselves.

But we decided to do something we had never done before in such a situation: Sing hymns to God. It wasn't what we felt like doing. But we did it anyway. I call it prayer conditioning. As we let our prayers of praise float to God, the air inside the car was reconditioned. Evil moods and atmospheric poison vanished. We were back on God's road again.

Praise can keep a bad situation from getting worse. It is a discipline to practice not only when we feel like doing it, but even when we don't.

There are those who would say that this is a form of dishonesty, covering up your real feelings. I felt the same way when I first heard this teaching about praise. But while there is danger of losing our honesty, I have come to believe that we do not have to sacrifice honesty when we praise God in all circumstances. It is a question of whether we want to build our honesty on our feelings, or on our faith. Feelings are an unreliable guide. I have found that if I act on my faith, my feelings will usually follow in line. By praising God in faith, I am no longer quite such a slave to my feelings.

Q2: What do you think? Is it a sign of faith or phoniness to praise God even in hard times? Have you ever tried this? What was the result? How can you keep both honesty and praise in such situations?

Twice, during my first pastorate, I found my job threatened. The first time, I suffered terribly from self-pity ("nobody wants us") and from anxiety that ate away at my stomach.

But by the time the second threat hit, I had decided to give my life to God and try to live for His glory, not for my own advancement. Though I was imperfect at it, one thing did get through to me: If I have given myself to God, there is no point in defending myself or protecting my position. I can trust God.

To ward off self-pity and anxiety, I said to myself: "Praise you, God. I don't know what you have in mind for me. A year has gone by without the least hope of a new position. But I trust that You are working this situation out. I am ready to serve and praise You even if You take me out of the pastorate altogether. Thank you, Lord, for giving me this new aim in life." As I reminded myself of God's faithful love for me, peace and joy would replace fear and confusion. It was this way of praising God that got me through the second time of job insecurity without a recurrence of ulcers, though I fell from this complete trust many times.

Building a Praise Vocabulary

Expressing love and praise requires a special vocabulary, and, like learning a foreign language, it can take a little time to become familiar with the new words. Here are some suggestions for growing in praise:

- Develop a list of the titles or names of Jesus; meditate on them and speak them out prayerfully.
- Express appreciation for the mighty acts of God, both in your own life, and in history.
- Meditate on the qualities of the character of Jesus and the Father in Heaven.
- Post praise-filled scriptures on the walls or doors of your house as a constant help to learn the vocabulary of praise.
- Write your own psalms of praise.
- Sing along to your favorite praise recordings.
- Learn simple praise songs that can be easily memorized, and sing them while you drive to work.
- Weave praise (spoken or sung) into your daily quiet time.
- Meet regularly with other Christians who have the praises of God in their hearts. Sing together in Bread group meetings.
- Memorize Psalms.

Q3 Which of these suggestions have not yet found their way into your praise vocabulary? Try some new approaches, both in private, and in the group—and see what happens!

Scripture Study for Chapter Thirteen

- **Psalm 63** (David offers a sacrifice of praise.)

- **Psalm 146** (Praise grows as faith grows.)

- **Habakkuk 3:17-19** (Habakkuk's sacrifice of praise)

- **Acts 16:19-34** (Paul and Silas give their praise sacrifice.)

- **Ephesians 5:18-20** (Paul preaches what he practiced.)

- **1 Thessalonians 5:16-18** (...in all things.)

It is as though we had put our clothes in a washing machine and added the soap, but then failed to turn the machine on.

14

Confession of Sin

Staying close to God is not easy. Our relationship with God is connected to our relationships with other people. We cannot get away from this principle.

Anyone who claims to be in the light but hates his brother is still in the darkness. Whoever loves his brother lives in the light, and there is nothing in him to make him stumble. But whoever hates his brother is in the darkness and walks around in the darkness; he does not know where he is going, because the darkness has blinded him. (1 John 2:9-11)

The way we treat other people can grieve the Holy Spirit, so that we lose the sense of God's closeness (Ephesians 4:29-32). This sense—what Mme. Sheikh called "glory"—is what the apostle John called "living in the light," while the apostle Paul called it "keeping in step with the Spirit" (Galatians 5:25).

Q1: Try to think of some times when you had that sense of "living in the light," and then lost it. Is there anything you do that consistently prevents you from "keeping in step with the Spirit?"

In many ways our relationship with God is like our relationship with people we live with. We can do things that alienate us from them. For example, my friend, psychologist Steve Sandage, tells this story in his book *To Forgive Is Human:*

My wife, Danielle, and I locked horns in one of our worst arguments shortly after moving into a new apartment. We reached an impasse after several minutes of verbal sparring, so I offered a psychological interpretation of what I thought her problem was (spouses of counselors will know what I'm talking about). Danielle found my interpretation about as helpful as the flu. She strongly counseled me to reserve my own counsel for my paying clients. Then she stormed out of the bedroom, slamming the bathroom door behind her to shut out my lecturing. I hated her getting the last word!

Several minutes passed with Danielle in the bathroom and me sitting on the bed stewing. Then I heard the knob on the bathroom door rattle. It rattled again. I remembered noticing the day before that the bathroom door would stick when closed all the way and realized Danielle was stuck in the bathroom. I wish I could say there was something besides joy in my twisted heart at that moment. Glee might be closer to the truth. I knew how to get the door unstuck but was in no big hurry to do so. I began to laugh on one side of the door, and could hear Danielle laughing on the other side. As I opened the door to the bathroom, laughter opened the door to forgiveness.[1]

The Problem of Garbage

Steve was rescued from disaster by a chance incident that brought laughter. But more often, laughter does not clear the air. Many of us live in families where sins and wrongs have piled up over the years until everyone in the family is living in piles of spiritual garbage. From this garbage emanates bad feeling and bitterness. The garbage can range from a lifetime of bickering and quiet resentment to the grossest forms of satanic bondage and ritual abuse.

Garbage that has piled up in us and our households can usually be cleaned away through confession of sin. Such confession takes great courage but it has equally great rewards. The courage can come from faith in Jesus. He encourages us to admit to our faults and ask forgiveness from God and other people. The apostle John wrote:

If we claim to have fellowship with him (God) yet walk in the darkness, we lie and do not live by the truth. But if we walk in the light, as he is in the light, we have fellowship with one another, and the blood of Jesus, his Son, purifies us from all sin.

If we claim to be without sin, we deceive ourselves and the truth is not in us. If we confess our sins, he is faithful and just and will forgive us our sins and purify us from all unrighteousness. If we claim we have not sinned, we make him out to be a liar and his word has no place in our lives. (1 John 1:6-10)

Long before scientists discovered that blood cleanses out impurities from our bodies, the Bible told of a spiritual power, the blood of Jesus, that can cleanse our hearts of sin and guilt. This invisible power can purify our inner nature of the impurities that accumulate there.

But according to the apostles, the blood of Jesus does not work until we confess our sins. When we don't confess them, it is as though we had put our clothes in a washing machine and added the soap—the atoning death (or blood) of Jesus. But then we fail to turn the machine on, so that the agitator works the soap into the clothes to get them clean.

Yet confession is risky business, because we have to lower our guard, trust God with our reputation, and take responsibility for our mistakes. This becomes possible when we are learning to put our reputation in God's hands. It is all part of trusting God—faith working through love.

Seasons of Great Awakening—A Lesson

From past seasons of spiritual awakening, when the Holy Spirit has been especially active throughout the world, there come many illustrations of how God invites confession of sin. The Holy Spirit strongly invites people to get rid of their spiritual garbage. For example, Jonathan Goforth described what happened when the Holy Spirit convicted two church leaders:

Then an elder stood up and said to another elder, who was seated on the platform: "In the session meetings it was always my bad temper that was the cause of trouble. Please forgive me." And the elder who was thus addressed cried back: "Please don't say any more. I'm just as much at fault as you are. It's you who should forgive me."[2]

To those who are still trying to clothe themselves with fig leaves, this process may be humiliating, embarrassing and painful. Yet when the Holy Spirit is at work, people rush to be the first to do it! Past seasons of spiritual awakening are full of stories of hundreds of people lining up to publicly confess deeply personal sins! They suddenly see that they can be clean, and they want cleanness with all their hearts.

Well then, what should we do?—wait for a spiritual awakening to come along so that we can be swept up in a tide of purification?

During these times of "awakening," God reminds us of what is always true, that He wants us to take off our fig leaves and put on His white garments. Trusting Jesus means that we stop justifying ourselves. Then we can look fair and square at our sin because it no longer blinds us.

Q2: For decades, Western culture has rejected the idea of confessing sin, because it has rejected the idea of sin. What do you see as the consequences of this twentieth-century trend, and do you think Christians should go along with it?

Dealing With the Darkness

Living in the light means the opposite of what we often think it means. Most people seem to think that it means going to church and pretending that there is nothing wrong with us. Smiling at each other, they speak wonderful words of faith and victory, as though they couldn't possibly have any problems or sin—after all, they are Christians!

In reality, they have been thinking wretched thoughts all day long, thoughts they are too embarrassed to admit to. They are consumed with bitterness against people who have wounded them. They are feeling as far from God as they ever felt when they were unbelievers. But somehow these secrets seem out of place in the company of the holy, so they don't admit to them when they are in church. Trapped in this dilemma, many Christians don't bring the darkness to light.

While it is important for us to confess our faith in God's promises, confessions of faith must never be done *in lieu of* confession of sin. If confession of faith becomes a cover-up for sin, we will end up like the Pharisee Jesus used as an example of self-righteousness:

> The Pharisee stood up and prayed about himself: 'God, I thank you that I am not like other men—robbers, evildoers, adulterers—or even like this tax collector. I fast twice a week and give a tenth of all I get.'
>
> But the tax collector stood at a distance. He would not even look up to heaven, but beat his breast and said, "God, have mercy on me, a sinner." (Luke 18:11-13)

Who among us cannot think of political and religious leaders who have been forced to admit to deeply embarrassing sins that discredited them before their stunned and disappointed followers. Is this pattern of sleaze and corruption inevitable? Are we doomed to be forever disappointed by each other and by the people we trust to lead us?

No, there is a pattern all can learn to follow: voluntary confession through the guidance of the Holy Spirit. This is especially appropriate during the sacrament of holy communion:

> A man ought to examine himself before he eats of the bread and drinks of the cup. ...If we judged ourselves, we would not come under judgment. When we are judged by the Lord, we are being disciplined so that we will not be condemned with the world. (1 Corinthians 11:28,31)

In other words, we should regularly seek the Lord, asking Him to show us where we have entered into the kind of self-deception that the apostle John warned us about, where we start walking in darkness, and the darkness blinds us so that we cannot even see that we are walking in darkness! We walk farther and farther away from God without realizing it—and all the time calling ourselves Christians.

Q3: What good does it do to admit to sins and mistakes? Can it do any harm? Evaluate this commandment of the apostles based on experiences when you tried to admit to a sin.

Moving Through to Healing

Confession of sin is one of the most difficult parts of the Christian life. Therefore, it is one of the most ignored, even among Christians who get the other parts right. Many people believe that it is adequate to simply come to church, read a printed prayer out of the church bulletin, and then be done with it.

In my experience, however, this liturgical solution does not often produce the cleanness that God intended. We should not be satisfied with our confession of sin until we have arrived at the scriptural goal: healing in our relationships with God and other people. The desolation, the garbage inside us should be washed away, and we should sense that we are ready for a fresh start with God and with our loved ones. "Confess your sins to each other and pray for each other, so that you may be healed" (James 5:16). Healing is the goal. We should test our confession of sin to see if it is producing this result. Do we feel joy at the end of it? Do we sense a new friendship growing up with other people? Do we know in our hearts that the darkness is gone?

Doing It Right

There are right ways and wrong ways to confess sin.

To whom should we confess a sin? The guideline I have used is this: Confess a sin to God alone if it is a sin that hurts God alone. If other people are involved in the offense, get right with those other people, too. If it is a sin against the public (a violation of public trust, for example), then the sin should be confessed in public.

What is the right way to confess a sin? Many people, in process of confessing a sin, make so many excuses and explanations that they end up canceling out the apology. When you have violated a relationship, don't give any excuses or explanations. Admit the mistake and ask forgiveness. "I really trampled on your feelings. Could you find it in your heart to forgive me?"

Don't run yourself down. Being down on yourself doesn't help either you or the other person. What other persons want to know is that you are aware that you hurt them, you regret it because you value them, and you would like to learn how to relate to them differently. The purpose of the confession is not to bask in self-condemnation, but to restore a relationship clogged with spite, hurt, guilt and repressed anger.

Restoring the relationship is always possible with *God*, who offered a sacrifice of atonement to prove His will to forgive. On the other hand, most *people* need a little time to deal with the wounds inflicted on them. There is no guarantee that they will ever grant forgiveness, let alone grant it immediately. A person who has been hurt by chronic sin habits for decades may not be ready for reconciliation in a day. Restoring a relationship may take more than a quick confession of sin. It may require the slow rebuilding of trust through consistent repentance and change. When the other person is not ready to grant forgiveness, pray that God would grant them the power to be rid of bitterness and mistrust. Believe that God can restore all things in His time.

Q.4: Do you see any relationships in your life where spiritual garbage has accumulated and never been cleared away? How would you begin the garbage removal?

In the next chapter, we will look into the other side of the equation, and ask what God can do for us to help us forgive those who have wounded us, even when they have not asked for forgiveness.

Scripture Study for Chapter Fourteen

- **Psalm 32** (Seeds of blessing in confession of sin)
- **Psalm 51** (David's confession of sin)
- **1 John 1** (Confession gets the blood of Jesus flowing.)
- **1 John 2:1-14** (The goal: to be able to walk in the light)
- **Luke 18:9-14** (Righteousness versus self-righteousness)
- **James 5:16** (Confession leads to healing.)

Forgiveness cuts through the knots.

15

Crumpling the IOUs

Jesus told many parables to help us see ourselves the way God sees us. One of them concerned a servant who owed his master a staggering debt of ten million dollars. His master forgave him the debt, absorbing the loss himself. The next day, the servant went up to a friend, who happened to owe him $20. He demanded payment immediately, or he would take his friend to court. The master heard of his servant's unforgiving attitude, decided not to forgive his servant after all, and threw him into prison (Matthew 18:15-35).

The debt I owe God is of the ten million dollar variety. The debt others owe me is usually of the $20 variety. God forgave my debt through Jesus. Now He wants His forgiveness to make me more forgiving, like Jesus. "A new commandment I have given you, that you love one another as I have loved you" (John 13:34). "As the Lord has forgiven you, so you also must forgive" (Colossians 3:13).

Is This Bad News Or What?

Not only does this parable have a bad ending. It has an offensive moral. Forgive! Why should I? Do I enjoy being wounded, slandered or knocked around? Is there any consolation in being the recipient of people's jokes, crimes or stupidities? Only one: the privilege of holding the offender in debt. Now God blames me for wanting to do this one thing: getting even.

Isn't getting even right and fair? Is God against justice? Doesn't the Bible say, "An eye for an eye, a tooth for a tooth" (Deuteronomy 19:21)? People should be made to pay! It balances the scales, right?

Before Jesus came, everything was clear. A person who committed a crime had to pay back the moral debt to the victim. This was only just. When the debt was repaid, the law (*God's* law, mind you) was fulfilled.

Then God sent Jesus, who paid a debt He didn't owe, so that we would not have to pay the debt we did owe God. This was not just; it was merciful. Now there is a new law that replaces the old one. The apostle James described it:

> Speak and act as those who are going to be judged by the law that gives freedom, because judgment without mercy will be shown to anyone who has not been merciful. Mercy triumphs over judgment! (James 3:12-13)

Yes the Old Testament says, "An eye for an eye; a tooth for a tooth." But the New Testament replies, "If you do not forgive men their sins, your Father will not forgive your sins" (Matthew 6:15). This is one of those areas in which the New Covenant surpasses and replaces the Old: "In speaking of a new covenant, he (God) treats the first as obsolete" (Hebrews 8:13).

The rule of thumb I use is this. I look at the Old Testament through the window of the New. This is one area where the Old and New Covenants differ: in the principle of forgiveness. The "eye for an eye" passage does not apply among Christians, because the New Covenant recommends mercy.

Why God Introduced the New Law

Bitterness is a very expensive pleasure. One man I know is still stewing over injustices done to him years ago by "church people." He has never forgiven them. Unforgiveness has turned his whole life sour.

A woman I once counseled had a habit of bringing up offenses against her husband that reached back to their wedding day. She excused herself: "My problem is that I have such a good memory!" But God calls it what it is: not a good memory, but an unforgiving heart. And He says, *If you have such a good memory, remember what you, the servant, owed me, the Master.*

I once counseled four boys who were in jail on a felony charge. Three of them were let off on probation. One was imprisoned for three years. As I continued to visit the one in prison, I could see bitterness taking over and becoming the dominant force in his life. Revenge was the only thing he could get excited about. Bitterness became his consuming passion—and his real jail cell.

Binding and Loosing

The scriptures speak of "binding and loosing." What appropriate language! People are tied up in knots, tangled in webs of guilt, bitterness and moral confusion. The tangles loop out to ensnare others, who fall into the webs they spin. In Ruanda the Hutus kill the "verminous" Tutsis. The Tutsis slaughter the "treacherous" Hutus. Pretty soon no one is left alive. All are caught in webs of hate and revenge.

Though we love to watch movies about it, revenge is a deceptive passion that has no place in Christ's abundant life. It will trap us, and cause us to veer from The Target. Jesus gives us, not sympathy for our bitterness, but a hard-nosed discipline that heals. He tells us to forgive those who have hurt us. "If you don't forgive them, God won't forgive you." Wow! That's heavy! That's the "binding" part of "binding and loosing." But God has to be severe with us at this point because the alternative—slaughtering each other with revenge—is much worse. The way out of the web of hate is through the discipline of forgiveness. Forgiveness cuts through the knots.

Revenge, a Deceptive Passion

I once knew a who had a reputation as a social activist. One day he invited me to a bar; he wanted to talk to me. I was a little nervous about this because I could tell he had already had too much to drink. But I agreed. The bar we went to happened to be owned by an Asian. The activist held a deep-seated grudge against Asians, as I was soon to discover. When the bartender refused to serve him (because he had already had too much to drink), he became abusive. He shouted out that he was going to sue the owner for racial prejudice. Then he asked me to be his witness in a legal suit.

I refused. I could see that his real enemy was not the bar owner, who didn't know him from Adam. It was the resentment in his own heart, eating away at him, threatening his marriage, destroying his ministry to the poor, and filling him with alcohol. I saw, more clearly than ever, the foolishness of unforgiveness. The bar owner could not have cared less whether my friend forgave him or not. Unforgiveness did not hurt the bar owner. But it was destroying my friend's life.

Q.1: *What do you do when resentment and bitterness have a grip on you? Have you found any clues for handling situations where you have been deeply wounded?*

The Power To Forgive

At heart it is a question of power. Do we have power to forgive? Jesus said to His disciples, "Receive the Holy Spirit. If you forgive the sins of any they are forgiven; if you retain the sins of any they are retained" (John 20:22-23). Through the Holy Spirit Jesus gave to them God's power to loose people from bondage and guilt, if they chose.

This type of forgiveness can be unilateral. You and I can give forgiveness to those who have hurt us, whether or not they have sought it from us. So far as we know, no one ever asked Jesus for forgiveness. But Jesus conveyed forgiveness unilaterally (Luke 23:34). The Holy Spirit gives us the same power. We can ask God to make us a channel of forgiveness to the very persons we most resent. In our prayer time, we can pray for their forgiveness, just as Jesus told us to do (Matthew 5:44). We can overcome evil with good. Evil cannot master us when we remain in Christ, striving to have His heart.

Uncovering Roots of Hurt

Jesus told us to forgive "from the heart." Our hearts are full of old memories of wrongs and hurts others have committed against us. These memories may be so painful that we take care to keep them closed off most of the time. Yet the memories remain, and do a great deal of damage in innumerable ways. Many who minister healing today say that forgiveness can cleanse those old hurts, and lead to inner healing that is profoundly liberating.

Carla and I once invited a teenage girl to live with us for a season. I will call her Kim. Kim was a troubled girl. She was staying with us because she had threatened her adoptive father with a knife, and was no longer welcome at home. After several weeks, we discovered that Kim was having nightmares. She dreamed repeatedly of someone coming at her to attack her.

We wanted to help Kim, so we asked if she would mind if we counseled and prayed with her about the dreams. As we came together, my wife and I asked Kim if she could remember any situation that her dreams reminded her of. She reminisced about her years in the orphanage, when she had been attacked and sexually abused. She relived that scene in her imagination, though it was a very frightening and painful memory. She brought it to Jesus.

We asked Jesus to enter the closet where that memory was stored, and clean it out. Jesus helped her see the situation in a new way. He comforted her and strengthened her, so that she was released from fear. Soon Kim was able to see the perpetrator as someone in need of Christ's love. She could see that he was all tied up in moral confusion, and in passions beyond his control. She forgave him, and asked Jesus to love him as He loved her. That closet was swept clean. The result? She stopped having nightmares. Something had been healed.

Dennis and Matthew Linn, in their book, *Healing Life's Hurts*, wrote that forgiveness is the one essential ingredient in overcoming psychological trauma at the heart of so much of what ails us.

We know that we have taken Christ's hand to heal a memory not when we can say, "That's O.K." but when we go through the struggle to forgive those who hurt us. This is the same struggle with feelings of denial, anger, bargaining, and depression that the dying experience in forgiving God, others, and themselves for their declining life.... We are healed when we can say not "That's O.K." but "I forgive you for hurting me because it brought so much growth that I'm grateful it happened."[1]

Forgiveness is what keeps temporary hurts from becoming permanently crippling to the spirit.

Yes, But...

Forgiveness may sound good in a discussion, but when we are
faced with doing it, questions spring up. For instance: "Do I have to
go up to a person and say 'I forgive you?' Wouldn't that be pre-
sumptuous?"

I once had a girl-friend who said that to me. Our relationship
had deteriorated with a harsh blowup. A few days later, she ap-
proached me and said: "I forgive you." Yet she was an ice-berg after
that, and I knew that nothing was resolved. I didn't even know what I
had done that deserved to be forgiven. At that point, forgiveness
didn't seem like a very good idea.

Jesus says that we are to forgive *from the heart*. When we have
done this, it will show in our smile, our touch, our way with people.
The real issue, then, is the condition of our heart.

Forgiveness results from an inner struggle in which we ask God
for His perspective about people who have hurt us. Sometimes He
shows us their struggle or He gives us His grief over them. Our job is
to give up our heart to Him in the middle of our woundedness, and
see what God says to us about it. Forgiveness, in other words, grows
out of an honest conversation with God. Once we have let Him
change our heart, then we are in a position to forgive from the heart.

*Q2: Think of someone who has hurt you. How can you yield to
God the wounds in your heart? Have you ever experienced
God's power to change your perspective toward people who
have hurt you? If you have, tell it to the group.*

Forgiving Evil People

A second question: Does forgiveness imply that we have to forget and ignore the dangers and evils we deplore? A woman once
came to me with this quandary: another woman had been making a
play for her husband. For several months, this other woman had
caused upset in their household, though they had a stable marriage
and trusted each other to be faithful. Still, it caused a strain to have

such a woman about, who continued to take advantage of their friendship. Finally, in exasperation, the couple told her that unless she quit flirting, they would sever all ties with her.

The warning didn't change a thing, so they cut her off. After they did this, she tried to push their guilt button, insisting that Christ commanded them to forgive her! She used this argument to keep up her flirting! They didn't buy it.

Forgiving a person does not mean that we cannot deliver a serious word of correction when it is due. Nor does it mean that we are required to expose ourselves to continued dangers from those who chronically hurt everyone around them. Jesus said there are times when we are justified to "shake the dust off our feet," (Matthew 10:14). Paul said something similar: "Do not regard him as an enemy, but warn him as a brother" (2 Thessalonians 3:15).

When we have forgiven people from the heart, we gain God's perspective to correct them in love, discipline them, or just let bygones be bygones, whatever God would have us do.

Q3: Whom do you need to forgive? Name the people who have hurt you in the past. Then jot down how you can demonstrate forgiveness to them. Privately pray for those people that the Lord will release and bless them. Try to picture them as needy people, receiving God's love. Experience God's mercy toward them. Pray for each other in group, wherever people struggle with unresolved hurt.

Scripture Study for Chapter Fifteen

- **John 20:19-23** (The Holy Spirit gives power to forgive.)

- **Hebrews 12:12-15** (The root of bitterness can damage not only ourselves, but the people around us.)

- **Colossians 3:12-15** (Christ's example strengthens us.)

- **Matthew 18:15-35** (Christ's teaching shows the way.)

- **Luke 17:3-4** (Forgiveness is never inappropriate.)

- **Ephesians 4:29-32** (The Holy Spirit is grieved when we fail to forgive.)

Mary poured expensive oil of nard over His head and feet.

16

Loving God with Money

Probably the last area we are willing to put under God's control is our money—or perhaps I am letting my Scottish heritage show through! This unruly part of life can be harnessed and used to help us grow in faith and love.

As we grow *in faith*, our faith will affect our attitude toward money. In our recent book, Prayer That Shapes the Future, Brad Long and I tell of Archer Torrey, who gave up his position as head of the Anglican seminary in Seoul, Korea to found Jesus Abbey, a prayer center in the Korean mountains. There people would learn to study God not just by reading books about Him, but by relying on Him. Let me repeat the story Brad told from memory:

Once I accompanied Archer to a conference in Seoul at the 8th Army Retreat Center. On the way, he told me that the Abbey had run out of money for daily operations. He asked me to join him in praying for provision....

About midway through the conference I saw an American military man privately come up to Archer and hand him a stack of Korean money about a forth of an inch think. I was amazed. Our prayer experiment had worked. But this was just the beginning.

The next day, a woman gave a report of some mission work that was being done in another part of Korea. She had urgent financial needs that, unless they were met immediately, would close down the work. After her plea for help, we all went into prayer for this situation. I watched Archer, who seemed to be struggling with some issue in his spirit. Then, during lunch, I watched him come up to this woman, pull out the stack of bills he had just received, and hand it over to her.

I could not believe it. He had just given away what I was sure was God's provision for the Abbey. I had touched another principle of prayer, but I did not understand it or like it: "the obedience of faith" (Romans 1:5, RSV). I continued my prayer for provision for the Abbey, but really did not expect anything else to happen.

On the last day of the event, as we were leaving, a Korean woman came up to Archer and...pulled out of her purse a stack of 10,000-won bills several times thicker than the first stack, and she handed it to Archer. She said, "This is for the Abbey in thanks for what God has done!"[1]

Archer had learned to trust God. It affected the way he handled money. He consulted God about his money, both its inflow and its outflow.

If we seek God's kingdom and righteousness, God will care for our basic needs. Or at least He will provide a way for us to do so. Compare 2 Thessalonians 3:10—"If a man will not work, he shall not eat" with Deuteronomy 8:18—"It is God who gives you the ability to produce wealth."

But if you do not believe in God's care, it will be difficult to give that hard earned money away. Even if you have all the possessions you could possibly want, you will want to store up all your money as a hedge against future catastrophe. You will never put yourself in a position of dependence on God.

Q1: Have you ever been in a situation of serious financial need? Did you respond out of faith or unbelief? Looking back on it, can you see any ways that God provided for your needs or taught you a lesson through the shortage?

Money for Love

As we grow *in love*, our love will also affect the way we treat money.

This is how we know what love is: Jesus Christ laid down his life for us. And we ought to lay down our lives for our brothers. If anyone has material possessions and sees his brother in need but has no pity on him, how can the love of God be in him? (1 John 3:16-17)

God is taking aim at our grasping, covetous hearts, which cause the rich to get richer and the poor to get poorer.

Mary, the sister of Lazarus, came to Jesus and poured expensive oil of nard over His head and feet. This was her way of honoring a guest. It was an act of sacrificial love, because Mary probably had to sell something of great value to buy that oil. But one of Jesus' followers (Judas Iscariot) said indignantly: "It could have been sold and the money given to the poor." Jesus replied, "the poor you have with you always." He was drawing attention from the money itself to the love in Mary's heart, which was far more important to God.

Q2: Analyze your own motivation in giving money away. What have been your reasons for parting with your hard-earned cash? Compassion for hurting people? Altruism? Jesus' command to "seek first His kingdom?" Guilt: you can't say no when someone asks you for something?

Where Is Your Heart?

Jesus said, "Where your treasure is, there your heart will be also" (Matthew 6:21) Some people say, "I will devote myself to making a lot of money and then I will wisely invest it and become rich. Then I will be able to do more good for God."

Maybe. The problem with money is that it has power to become an idol. Paul wrote: "The love of money is a root of all kinds of evil" (1 Timothy 6:10).

One of the most misunderstood parables in the Bible is the parable of the ten talents (Matthew 25:14-30). A master gave one of his servants ten coins. The servant invested them and the money grew. A second servant received five coins, which he also invested. The master gave a third servant one coin, which he buried in the ground. The master commended the first two, but condemned the third, because the third did not make his money grow.

This parable is often interpreted as a story about money, or about "time, talents and treasures." But the word "talent" is nothing more than a happenstance: the Greek word *talentia* was the name of a gold coin worth $10,000. Is God really saying that He is offended when we fail to invest our money wisely? No, this is a parable of God's kingdom. It makes a comparison between money and something else.

It deals with the treasures of the Kingdom of God, which Jesus gave His servants when He ascended on high. At that time, Jesus didn't give His disciples coins, or time or talents. He gave them the treasures of the New Covenant: the blood of Jesus, the Holy Spirit, the authority of the believer, the hope of the gospel. These are the treasures that this parable is talking about, not money.

The parable confronts us with an opportunity: to invest the things of Jesus into a world that doesn't have them yet. Put another way, we invest money in making God's love grow, rather than investing so much time making money that we ignore the things of God.

Giving, a Spiritual Gift

God does seem to prosper some people financially. These people may come into wealth because God wants to use them for a ministry of contribution guided by the Holy Spirit. Contribution is a spiritual gift—a ministry God gives to certain people (Romans 12:8).

The story of *Fresh Bread* is an example of God's provision. At the start, the first 500 copies of the first Bread book were printed in 1976 by a local printer who "happened" to attend my church in Oregon at just the right time, and printed them for me free. Later God led me to self-publish 5000 copies of a revised version—and brought in the full $5000 for this purpose, some of it from people I didn't even know. More recently, the present printing of *Fresh Bread* was paid for with money by people who were led to give certain amounts, totalling exactly the costs of publication.

When the Holy Spirit is truly motivating us to give, we will probably notice three things.

First, the motive will be love, not compulsion (2 Corinthians 9:7). A man I know once joined a church. Soon after that, a couple of members visited him to tell him that they expected him to give a certain percentage of his income to the church. They had even taken the trouble to find out what his income was, and what the correct contribution should be! When people try to get that kind of leverage into our pocketbooks, we are right in resisting. That kind of pressure can quickly kill the joy of giving—which is God's reward for Spirit-guided ministry.

Second, the Holy Spirit provides guidance in our contribution. The lives of men like Hudson Taylor and George Muller are filled with $308 needs met with contributions of $308. Often, their contributors did not know that their gift would fit an exact need. They were simply obedient and God worked out the proper amount.

Third, the Holy Spirit encourages faithfulness in the way we use money. God wants us to get into regular patterns of giving to works that He cares about. Giving guided by the Holy Spirit is not as impulsive as we might think it would be. For example, when Paul took up a collection from the Gentile Christians for the persecuted Jerusalem church, this was what he advised:

> On the first day of every week, each of you is to put something aside and store it up, as he may prosper, so that contributions need not be made when I come. (1 Corinthians 16:2)

Paul was not planning to come to Corinth, deliver an inspiring plea for money, whip people into a frenzy and hope for a big haul. This type of practice ignores one important fact about the Holy Spirit: He is trying to develop in us the fruit of the Spirit, like faithfulness and self-control. In my own giving, there is a place for regular tithes to my church, and also special gifts when the Lord clearly guides me about a specific project or ministry.

Is Tithing Legalistic?

Some say we should tithe (give the first 10% of our income), whereas others say that tithing is just for the Old Testament. The best basis for tithing comes from the example of Abraham, who tithed to the priest Melchizedek (Genesis 14:20). Abraham is not seen as an example of Old Testament law, because he predated the Mosaic law. Abraham is an example of faith, and that is why Paul lifted him up as a model for Christians to emulate. The book of Hebrews agrees, using Abraham as a model for tithing, and Melchizedek as a forerunner or model of Christ (Hebrews 7:1-10).

On the other hand, the first Christians felt that the New Covenant was far better than the Old. It was inconceivable that their response to God's New Covenant love would be less than that of the Jews. You don't read about any New Testament Christian tithing his income. Rather, they gave everything they had to the Church and received back as any had need. The principle that guided them is clarified by Paul: "He who gathered much had nothing left over, and he who gathered little had no lack" (2 Corinthians 8:15).

This practice of counting everything as the Lord's continued among Christians for centuries. In the second century, Irenaeus wrote: "Jews give a tenth of their goods to God; Christians give everything they have (and not just a little part) for the use of the Lord, that is, to the Church for the poor, giving freely and with joy because they hope for goods of a higher order."[2]

Tertullian, in the third century, wrote: "We do not think of goods as private. We who are in communion in heart and spirit do not hold back anything from the communion of goods. Everything among us is in common except marriage."[3]

In the fourth century, Augustine began his Christian walk by selling a considerable inheritance, in obedience to Christ. In the sixth century, Gregory dedicated his vast holdings, amassed as prefect (mayor) of Rome, to the poor and to the work of the Church. The early Church Fathers left us this witness: if our hearts are with Christ, our money will be His as well.

Q3: How much do you think you should devote to God's purposes, and how much to your own needs or wants? Should all Christians tithe? Try to come to a place where you have thought this through and have settled it in your own heart.

Should Christians Be Rich Or Poor?

Judging from books I find at Christian bookstores, some people believe that all Christians should be wealthy. Others look at Jesus and the disciples, note that they lived very simply, and teach that we should live in poverty or simplicity. Who is right?

Look at Paul's attitude:

I know what it is to be in need, and I know what it is to have plenty. I have learned the secret of being content in any and every situation, whether well fed or hungry, whether living in plenty or in want. I can do everything in him who gives me strength. (Phillipians 4:11-13)

Paul did not take a hard-line position either for wealth or for poverty. To him it was not money but freedom from money that characterizes the abundant life of Jesus. Money itself is neither a plus nor a minus. God calls us to provide for our families, and He provides us with means to do that. But that is not the purpose (or target) of the Christian life.

During times of financial tightness, I have learned important lessons in distinguishing between my wants and my needs. I have learned self-control, and how to identify my personal idols. My family also has benefited from these times. When we were forced to live simply, we all came together and everyone did their part to get us through the hard times. We "learned how to be in need."

Those times, in turn, helped us to appreciate God for the more abundant times, so that we could receive all things with thanksgiving. It is the combination of the two that has produced the kind of thankful hearts that Paul says is God's true goal with us (2 Corinthians 9:11-12).

Scripture Study for Chapter Sixteen

- **1 Corinthians 16:1-5** (Principles for a giving ministry)

- **2 Corinthians 8** (The rewards of a giving ministry)

- **2 Corinthians 9** (True giving results in thanksgiving to God.)

- **Malachi 3:6-12** (Giving is part of a covenant relationship with God.)

- **Deuteronomy 15:7-11** (God's concern is for our hearts as well as for the poor.)

- **1 Timothy 6:1-16** (Balancing our ministry to the poor with our responsibility to our families)

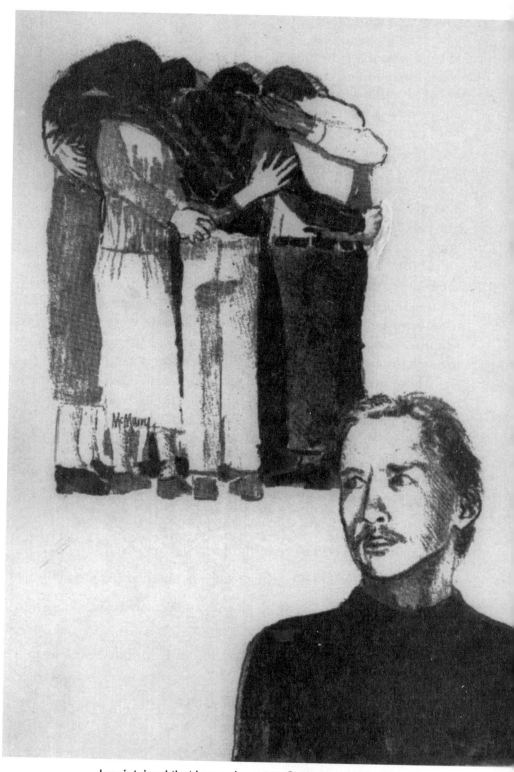

I maintained that I was closest to God when I was alone....

17

Why Jesus Has Churches

People become like their environment. We are immersed in a culture that maintains certain common beliefs, and there is a subtle pressure on everyone to conform to what the culture believes.

For example, when I was a young man, our culture believed that we live in a closed world where there is no spirit realm, where miracles are impossible, and angels and demons do not exist except in cartoons. Natural law had taken the place of God, and most people claimed to be content with that. We were just being modern.

In the 1970's all this began to change. A majority of Americans today—three out of four—believe that having a close relationship with God is very desirable.[1] Eighty percent believe that God works miracles today and that "there are spiritual forces that we cannot see but that affect the material world."[2] Miracles, released from their secret closets, have flooded the land. The skeptical worldview of the previous generation is now passe. We live in a postmodern world.

As one who grew up in the previous "modern" culture, I remember how that culture molded my beliefs. It is easier to see this by hindsight. I was convinced that God would never help me. Unbelief was everywhere, though we never labeled it such. It was just "the way things are." People who believed that God did things for you were thought to be either simple-minded or hopelessly mediaeval.

I was a product of an atheistic culture that paid lip-service to Christian faith. Most Americans believed the Bible only where it coincided with American culture. The "faith" part of faith working through love was nearly impossible for me. I was left with simple "love," the part of the pattern my culture could accept.

How a Culture Shapes Our Thoughts

Today I wonder: What subtle impact does our *present* culture have on my thinking? Our postmodern culture is not as atheistic as the other was, but it is an "anything goes," "everyone is equally right" sort of culture. This new set of values comes into our living rooms day in and day out.

My TV set has been, at times, an unwelcome influence. It has poured into my living room sub-Christian values and teachings, all under the guise of "entertainment." This is not surprising, considering the survey of 104 Hollywood TV executives that found that only 7% attended church, and most said that they saw their job as a means of spreading their standards and values into our culture.[3]

Their beliefs and values differ from values I hold as a Christian. Yet for a season I naively allowed this teacher to instruct my children in my own living room. After investing in cable TV, I, too, was soon wasting hours every day flipping through channels, imbibing one program after another. Finally the Lord challenged me to get a life, and I cut off my cable. Today I spend little time watching TV—at least compared to the five-hour daily average in America.

Looking back on those days, I can now see what a subtle impact the TV had on me. An unleashed TV set was demolishing my Christian principles at home, and teaching my children the opposite of what I wanted them to learn. We all accepted these things as normal. "It's just the way things are," we would say.

This is how a culture works. It has power, without our realizing, to give us a vision of who we are, what we can and cannot do, what we should hope to accomplish, what has value and what does not have value. All of this may or may not be of God. In our culture, there is much that is not of God, though many Christians hold to these values and beliefs because their TV sets speak into their ears five hours a day. It all happens subliminally.

Q1: Does your culture have any negative influences in your life that you have become aware of? Do you feel vulnerable to influences that seem unchristian to you? How can you protect yourself and your family from these influences?

In, Not of the World

Jesus does not tell us to build a wall around ourselves or our families, to cut off these negative influences. He says, "be *in* the world, but not *of* the world" (see John 17:14-19). Be among the influences, but do not be influenced by them! How is this possible?

Any high school student who has risked popularity by refusing to smoke a joint or have casual sex knows what I mean, as does any businesswoman who has decided not to cheat and still remain competitive. Yet Jesus says: live among the temptations—just don't yield to them. Frankly, this command seems impossible to obey.

God foresaw how hard this would be for us. So He provided not a wall of monastic separation, but an alternate culture to surround us. Look at the early Church, which had to learn to thrive in the midst of a blatantly pagan culture. How did they do it?

> They devoted themselves to the apostles' teaching and to the fellowship, to the breaking of bread and to prayer. Everyone was filled with awe, and many wonders and miraculous signs were done by the apostles. All the believers were together and had everything in common. Selling their possessions and goods, they gave to anyone as he had need. Every day they continued to meet together in the temple courts. They broke bread in their homes and ate together with glad and sincere hearts, praising God and enjoying the favor of all the people. And the Lord added to their number daily those who were being saved. (Acts 2:42-47)

They prayed together, ate together, were taught together, enjoyed one another's company, shared their possessions, praised God together and worshiped God every day. They became a Christian environment—in Augustine's words, "the society of new people." In this intensive Christian environment they could maintain their faith and love without removing themselves from the world, which God wanted them to transform by their very presence there.

We can form similar Christian environments. That is why Jesus has churches.

Q2: In what areas of your life do you see a need for the support of other Christians who earnestly seek God? How could you

profit from getting together with other Christians more fre-
quently? List four or five ways to share with the group, and
see if others have similar ideas.

Why Churches?

Of course, people have various ideas about what churches
should do for them. I have known churches that tried to be:
- a religious institution to preserve traditions,
- a political lobby to influence the government,
- a social club to provide rewarding friendships,
- a professional counseling or social work agency,
- an intellectual forum for the exchange of ideas.

More recently I asked myself: what does *God* want His Church
to be? The New Testament replies: God's Church is a family ("the
household of faith") where people are learning faith working through
love, the pattern of sound teaching. The New Testament gives two
reasons to come together regularly as Christians:
- to "hold fast the profession of our faith without wavering"
  (Hebrew 10:23, KJV) and
- to "spur one another on to love and good deeds" (Hebrews
  10:25).

There they are again: faith and love. And in order to maintain our
faith and love, we are to "not give up meeting together as some are in
the habit of doing..." (Hebrews 10:25).

Anyone who has ever tried to learn faith or love knows why a
Christian community is an essential part of Christian learning. I think
of a woman who used to be a real loner—she was addicted to soli-
tude. One day she caught Christian faith from a friend and became
excited about Jesus. But she could not talk about her growing faith or
meet with other Christians. She stayed in her house most of the
time, drinking heavily as she had done for years.

One day her family visited her. They ridiculed her faith.
Crushed by their cynicism, she decided that Christianity was more
than she could practice. She cut herself off from the few Christian
friends she had gained, becoming still more lonely—and drinking
more heavily.

Fortunately, she later realized her mistake. The Lord came into her life in fresh ways, and she was able to become a faithful member of my church. In church, she learned to come out of her isolation and to practice faith working through love. Later, her new family turned out to be even more important to her when her husband died an untimely death. She experienced a family's love in a way her biological family had never shown her.

There is little doubt that most Western churches are falling far short of the biblical picture of churches. The unchurched sense this lack of vision and are staying away from churches today.

Consider the following statistics: 65 percent of unchurched people claim the Christian faith is relevant to the way they live today, but only 27 percent believe that the church is relevant. And whereas 49 percent of the unchurched say that having a closer relationship with God is very desirable, only 13 percent say that being part of a local church is very desirable.[4]

Maybe what is needed is a complete retooling of the vision of what churches are for. The Bible can help.

What Can We Expect from a Church?

There are several ways a church can help us learn the pattern of faith working through love. All of these are non-manipulative. When we come to a church, we should not have people forcing us to do anything. Hopefully, they will have learned how to give us space to let God's Spirit do His work. According to 1 Timothy 4, the church should provide the following four non-manipulative ingredients for people who are seeking God:

1. Teaching and guidance. The apostle Paul told Timothy to "command and teach these things" (1 Timothy 4:11). The Bible contains God's "Kingdom of Heaven" culture, and the church is His means for transforming all the other cultures of the world. We are to allow Jesus' teaching to transform our minds (Romans 12:1).

But most people have a hard time simply opening their Bibles and living by them. That is why we have books 'like *Fresh Bread*, and pastors and teachers who help us understand the Bible from age to age. People have a right to evaluate whether their teaching is scriptural (Acts 17:11) and, again, we should not become overly dependent on teachers, but should learn to discern how the Holy Spirit uses God's word to teach us directly.

2. Exemplary people. Paul told Timothy, "Set an example for the believers in speech, in life, in love, in faith and in purity" (1 Timothy 4:12). Much of our learning comes from the example that mature people set for us. I think of a certain community of Christians I visited in 1972 in Michigan. There, 700 people were gathered in a gymnasium to worship God. How well I remember the excitement—their warm welcome, the expressions of faith that made God come alive, and the testimonies about miracles of God. It did wonders for me to visit that community—it showed me true Christian faith and love in action. Ever since then, I have had that picture in mind as a goal to strive for in my life and ministry. One good example is worth more than many books.

In most churches there are leaders: pastors, elders, teachers and deacons. They will probably not be perfect Christians, but they should be "mature in Christ" (Colossians 1:28 RSV, Philippians 3:15). They should have had several years of following the pattern of Christ and they should exemplify it. We cannot reduce Christian leadership to a set of professional tasks in a job description, nor can we ignore basic standards of godliness, because God holds leaders to those standards (Hebrews 13:7, 1 Thessalonians 5:12-13). Leaders cannot be perfect, but they must deal with their imperfections in the way God says, so that others may see how to do it.

3. Training in godliness. Paul told Timothy, "Physical training is of some value, but godliness has value for all things, holding promise for both the present life and the life to come" (1 Timothy 4:8). The church provides opportunities for new believers to learn how to pray, worship, interpret scripture, forgive sin, confess sin, express faith, bear testimony, exercise spiritual gifts—in short, learn the pattern of faith working through love. If a church gets people together for Sunday school discussions but never leads them to actually *try* any of the ways of Christ, it will have failed in its God-given purpose. In a Bread group, for example, each member can and should be challenged to try—during group meetings—the things Christ has commanded. Training in godliness means that people will learn by doing. Sometimes churches become embroiled in speculation and controversy. But Paul tells Timothy to stick to the divine training that leads to faith and love (1 Timothy 1:3-7, RSV).

4. Protection. Paul warned Timothy about harmful people and told him not to cave in to them, even if they were older than he was (1 Timothy 4:1-5). A church ought to be free of ridicule, gossip, abuse, threats, harshness and other hurtful patterns that make it hard for people to learn God's ways. One of the leaders' duties is to protect the flock from those who would harm it (Acts 20:28-31). A church ought to be a sanctuary—a *place of prayer* and a *safe haven.*

Before my conversion, I maintained that I was closest to God when I was alone in nature, camping. But in recent years, I feel closest to God when I am meeting "two or more in Jesus' name." Yes, even a loner like myself can long for the company of fellow Christians, and find God there among them.

Q3: Have your experiences of churches matched these four criteria from 1 Timothy 4? Also, evaluate your Bread group according to these criteria. Are there ways you could improve your group?

Q4: How do you feel about the idea of the church not as an institution but as a community of Christians helping each other know God? Are you ready to pay the price?

Scripture Study for Chapter Seventeen

- **1 Peter 4:1-11** (Temptations of a non-Christian environment)
- **John 17:1-26** (In the world, not of the world)
- **Romans 12** (No longer conformed to this world)
- **Hebrews 10:23-25** (Be together regularly...)
- **Acts 2:41-47** (...like the first disciples at Jerusalem.)
- **Ephesians 4:11-16** (The Church's calling: bringing people to maturity in Christ)

An aim is a point on the horizon toward which we steer our boat.

PART THREE:

CHRISTIAN LOVE

18
Loving People by Faith

The Christian recipe for Kingdom living, as we have been describing it, is faith working through love. This secret recipe, when applied to every area of life, can fill us to overflowing with good things. Yet this recipe for zoe life is not widely known or practiced. It is still largely the secret of a few connoisseurs. Many people believe in love, and try to practice it. Few seem to have put together the divine concoction of Christian faith mingled with Christian love.

Loving a "Loved One"

When Carla and I got married, she "loved" me for my artistic ability and I "loved" her for her musical ability. We had much in common, and we encouraged each other in our abilities. We had a "mutual need fulfillment" kind of love, rather than the faith-working-through-love pattern that Paul described.

A couple of years into our marriage, we discovered that in some ways we were not good for each other. Even in those highly respected areas of art and music there were problems. She resented me every time I trundled down to my potter's wheel in the basement instead of staying to talk with her, as I had done during courtship.

When she went off to direct the church choir, I was not delighted to be a good house-husband, staying home to care for our kids. Nor did I appreciate having to counsel my wife after a troublesome evening with some overly sensitive choir members. My many charming feelings toward my wife evaporated, leaving a sticky residue of resentment.

I might have said I no longer loved her.

"God, Make Him Like I Want"

My wife recognized how fragile our marriage was. She had hoped for a house built on rock—a stable, comfortable relationship in which both of us would meet the other's needs, and where she would keep abiding in the affectionate, romantic love of courtship. My failure to provide romance put her on the edge of anxiety. She did not believe that our relationship had depth, and she wanted to be more sure of my love. So she set about getting me to be the kind of husband she expected.

I don't blame her! However, Jesus did not say, "She who would build her house on a rock must hear my love commandments and get *her husband* to follow them."

"God, Make Me Like You Want"

One day, the Lord spoke to my wife in a quiet, gentle way and said, "Trust me with your marriage." Somehow or other, Carla recognized that faith and trust translated into love and honor. She should no longer try to manipulate me to love her. Rather, she should try to love me, and trust God to make it come out right. She made a love decision based on faith in God's word.

One of the first changes I noticed was that Carla stopped criticizing my sermons. Until that time, her anxiety had prompted her to point out the mistakes I had made and the people I had probably offended from the pulpit. Now she stopped being my homiletics (preaching) professor, and started being my lover and encourager.

Her change, in turn, altered my feelings toward her. I found that I could be more romantic toward my wife than towards a homiletics professor! As a result of Carla's faith working through love, I began to meet her needs. But this decision on my part was not a result of manipulation on her part. It was a result of her freeing love, a decision of faith. If she had waited for me to be everything she wanted me to be, she'd be waiting still, no doubt.

Nothing has helped our marriage more than this love decision Carla made several years ago. It is changing me from the cold-hearted and affectionless loner I used to be, into the moderately warm and occasionally romantic lover I am today. Carla is leaning on God to help her love a husband, faults and all.

Now as I look back, I can see that the false and flimsy idea of love with which we entered marriage has been replaced by a more mature love. A friend of mine put it this way: "For the first five years, we had marriage. Now we've got holy matrimony!"

Q1: Do you find yourself locked into a pattern of criticism and irritation with anyone—especially someone you live with? Are you prepared to accept the challenge of loving that person despite personal feelings about them?

Christian love is not a feeling, but a faith-decision. Since Jesus is the one who commands this decision, we have to believe in Him. By faith in Him we can be freed from our old commander: our self-centered feelings. We give love for the sake of Christ. "Be subject to one another out of reverence for Christ" (Ephesians 5:21). Feelings come and go. But Jesus is always there. To build our lives on His love commandments is to build our homes on the rock.

Let Love Be Your Target

Few Christians, at the beginning of their faith walk, appreciate love as the outcome of true faith. Most people think that God mainly commands us to love those who are closest to us, whom we call "our loved ones." They think that they love God and all humanity, and would be offended at the suggestion that they need to improve or broaden their love—to love people as God loves them. Few have made love their aim in life.

Yet the scriptures tell us to do just that: make love our Life's Target (1 Corinthians 14:1). An aim is a point on the horizon toward which we steer our boat. We may pass other points, yet love remains always before us, giving us our bearings and guiding us through the shoals all around.

Suppose, for example, that I have recently become aware of the ministry gifts of prophecy, tongues and healing, and I want others to become aware of these gifts, too. Yet I find that I am growing increasingly edgy toward people who do not accept these gifts. I get upset with them and gossip about them (in the guise of praying for them). If I have made love my aim, I must now admit that my life is going off course, just as the apostle Paul described (1 Corinthians 13:1, 2). I must stop trying to be so "charismatic" and recognize that God has a different priority for me at present: to love. Perhaps when I have grown in love, I will be in a better position to help others appreciate charismatic gifts like prophecy, tongues and healing.

Or suppose I have been deeply impressed with the needs of the poor. I am ready to give my life to end poverty, to equalize the distribution of the world's goods. Yet I find myself increasingly hostile toward all who do not share my passion. I hate rich people who are blind to the needs of the poor. I am beginning to believe that violence is the only way to wrest the world's goods from the rich and give them to the poor. Again, I must honestly admit that my life has gone off course. I should slow down my bandwagon for the poor until I can grow in the love of God. "Make love your aim."

Q2: *Is there anything in Christianity that is so important to you that you are willing to offend and hurt people to see it triumph?*

Love: the Fulfillment of All the Rest

In the end, love is the only ministry we have. It is our only Christian witness (John 13:35). Love was what the entire Old Testament was really about (Galatians 5:14). Love is the same thing as eternal life (1 John 3:14-15). Those who love show that they have been born again; those who do not show that they haven't (1 John 4:7-21).

God is not aiming only to get us to heaven. He is aiming to make us loving, so that we may fit into heaven. The love commandments cry out from every book of the New Testament. If God can turn us into genuine lovers, that is a conversion indeed.

Yet, to be truthful, most churches do not present to the world a picture of overflowing love. Why is that? I have heard some Christians object that love is not unique enough to be the aim of the Christian life. "After all, non-Christian people can love too," they say. "If love is all there is to the Christian life, how are we different from anybody else?" Of course, that is the point: Love is a language everybody understands, even when they can't understand Christianese.

Jesus came to show us what true love is and to give us the power, through faith, to be lovers of the unlovable. Jesus never hates anyone, but only the sin we commit against the law of love.

Before There Was *Agape*

Few of us have any idea of what the world was like before Jesus came, and how little genuine love there was. Prior to Jesus, the New Testament word *agape* (love) was scarcely ever used. Like today, people were interested in *philos* (brotherly love) and *eros* (sexual love). But this mysterious *agape* was a word almost without meaning until Jesus came to show us what it meant.[1]

Who, before Jesus, had thought of loving their enemies? Who had described love as a decision (or command), rather than as a warm or romantic feeling? This faith-love is an idea from another world. It is not human. It is hard for us even to imagine it. Yet through faith, *agape* is possible. Love is a decision of faith, guided by scriptures and empowered by the Holy Spirit.

I once struggled with resentment against some leaders of our churches whom I perceived to be using church money to support sexual immorality and goddess worship. I wasted a lot of time complaining and murmuring against these people and against the leaders of our denomination. One day I realized that complaining is not one of God's commandments, and God required me to begin praying for those very leaders. This call to prayer, to date, has involved more than 600 hours of intensive intercessory prayer, a sacrifice of love for people I have never met. I had to realize that murmuring against people reflects neither faith nor love.

Returning Evil with Good

When we lived in Scotland, we had some neighbors who seemed determined to pick verbal fights with us. We tied a clothesline to their fence one day, and they came around to tell us to get our clothesline off their fence. "It's tearing the fence down," they groused. The next week they came by to tell us to move our garbage can. "This is our spot; your spot is over there."

While I was fuming with judgment and anger against their pettiness, my wife was calmly packaging some cookies for them, and planning how we could have them over for tea. Again, I made the wrong decision, but Carla made the right one. After we had tea with those neighbors, we actually found them delightful. We learned that their coolness toward us had stemmed from a long line of former tenants who had been inconsiderate and unfriendly. They had assumed that we would be the same. Now a new friendship was begun. Carla had overcome a chain reaction of evil with a single act of kindness.

Luther's Love

Martin Luther, the Protestant Reformer, was faced with a love-decision. By prayer and preaching he attacked the evils of his day. After several years, his preaching caught on, and the people of Germany began to rally around him. Yet many had not studied the New Testament as he had. They did not see love as the aim of the Christian life. Some counseled the German authorities to kill "ungodly papists." When Luther rejected violence as a way of bringing about change, these men turned on him, calling him "Brother Easychair," and "Dr. Pussyfoot." In reply, Luther wrote to the governors of Germany:

These Alstedters revile the Bible and rave about the spirit, but where do they show the fruits of the spirit: love, joy, peace and patience? . . . Our office is simply preaching and suffering. Christ and the apostles did not smash images and churches, but won hearts with God's Word.2

Luther had made a love-decision. It helped to keep him on the right track in the midst of the most severe provocations. In this he followed the apostle Paul, who wrote: "Do not be overcome by evil but overcome evil with good" (Romans 12:21).

Q3: Most of us know at least one person who has genuinely loved us. Why not take a minute to think of some such person. Ask yourself: How did he or she show love to you? What did love consist of?

As I reflect on this question, I realize that those who loved me valued me. They treated me as an important person. To love is to value.

We can choose to place a high or a low value on others. Some time ago, my parents gave me a gold watch, an heirloom from my great uncle. I went to have it appraised. The appraiser quoted $500. But to me it was worth more than that. I did not sell the watch, but continue to care for it and keep it safe.

I can choose to do the same with people. Care. Not sell. God calls me to see worth and potential in them because they were bought with a price.

Q4: Is there anyone in your life you could value more highly than you do? What does it do to your estimation of them when you remember that they were "bought with a price?"

Scripture Study for Chapter Eighteen

- **Galatians 5:13-26** (Walk the love commandment by the Spirit.)

- **1 Corinthians 13:1-14:1** (Make love your target.)

- **1 John 4:7-21** (He who loves is born of God.)

- **Romans 12:14-21** (Overcome evil with good.)

- **John 13:34-35** (Love one another as I have loved you...)

- **2 Peter 1:3-11** (...to keep you from being an ineffective Christian.)

God wants to repair, restore and remodel us as a better house for the Lord....

19

Holiness and Virtue

Hold on! It's time for a reality check!

Love, love, love. Everyone believes in love. But if we are at all serious about practicing it, we will have to look at our dark side, and deal with it.

We Americans have been confronted recently by a host of public figures who did not understand this principle. They went along with the deception that our American culture widely accepts, that we can sin, but if we keep it private, it won't matter. These figures have been playing out morality plays written by God, and we are the audience who are supposed to learn something from them.

Virtue, a Working Definition of Love

True love is blocked in us by all kinds of unvirtuous passions: fear, impatience, resentment, jealousy, selfishness, anxiety, pride, ambition and sexual lust. It is easy to talk of love, until we are suddenly caught in the grip of these passions that put love out of the question, or twist love until it is barely recognizable.

Christian teaching frankly recognizes these distortions of love and deals with them, even when most people would prefer not to. When the New Testament speaks of love, it also speaks of holiness (the process of sin-cleansing) because sin is what destroys love. Holiness gives rise to virtues that give love its shape. Without virtues, love never takes any shape at all. It is hypocritical to speak of love when we are unwilling to speak also of holiness and virtue. If sin did not destroy love, I feel sure that God would not be against it.

Virtue is God's working definition of love. Without that working definition, we tend to make the word "love" mean whatever we want it to mean.

Q1: Are you willing to look at some of your own negative habits, to become more loving? If so, what is it in your life that most often prevents you from loving others—especially the members of your family, or anyone God has called you to love?

A Working Definition of Lust

As I reflect on this question, I find that these negative habits turn out to be: *other loves!* But in most cases, the Bible would not call them loves. It has another word, in Greek, *epithumia*: "desire, longing, passion, lust." False loves.

These false loves are of many types. Let me name a few—and if I use the word "lust," it is only to point out that this word has a much broader meaning in the Bible than it does today for most Americans.

For example, the Bible speaks of mammon, the lust for material possessions (Matthew 6:24). It speaks of the "lust of the eyes and the pride of life" (1 John 2:16), which many TV, movie and advertising moguls promote; or the lust for power, which psychiatrists say often drives young children to rebel against their parents. The confusing thing about lust is that it often fastens itself to something good. For example, God made sex good (Genesis 1:27-31). Yet lust can turn sex into an obsession that violates and destroys people. God made the material world good. But lust can turn it into a driving compulsion to buy or steal. Justice is the fountainhead of order and right living. Yet lust can turn it into a bitter search for vengeance. Lust can turn patriotism into a fanatical war machine, as in Nazi Germany. Filled with lust, a mother's love becomes smothering mothering.

Lust, in short, can fasten itself on to any hobby, profession, drug, ambition or person. It gains power when we look to these things to do for us what only God can do. These things take over and bring us under bondage. We become slaves of lust, not bondservants of God. And in every case, lust will masquerade as love. In pagan religion, it is often exalted to the status of formal worship.

"But I Love My Lusts"

Lust is the lure that attracts us to false targets. It takes so many different forms that it would be impossible to enumerate them all. A good share of the Christian life is spent discerning what are the lusts that have fascinated us so we can get rid of them. For if anything is clear in the Bible, it is that Christians are called to give up our lusts, to fight them as though they were our worst enemy.

Put on the Lord Jesus Christ, and make no provision for the flesh, to gratify its lusts. (Romans 13:14, RSV)

Let not sin therefore reign in your mortal bodies, to make you obey their lusts. (Romans 7:12, RSV)

Put off your old nature which belongs to your former manner of life and is corrupt through deceitful lusts, and be renewed in the spirit of your minds, and put on the new nature, created after the likeness of God in true righteousness and holiness. (Ephesians 4:22-24, RSV)

Sometimes it is a struggle even to know what our lusts are, let alone to get rid of them. They hide so cleverly, whispering to us of "love" and "our rights," and "happiness." Had we not the Holy Spirit and the written word of God, getting rid of them would be a hopeless task, for our culture actively promotes them, and our lusts are, as Paul wrote, "deceitful." When we are pursuing them, we believe ourselves to be happy, but in the end, lusts destroy us under a heavy weight of disappointment and bondage.

What Is Wrong with Sin?

Most Americans believe that we should not have to confront our sin. We are in denial about it. For example, just in the sexual area, cohabitation, adultery, homosexuality and pornography are all considered to be more or less acceptable or inevitable. We shrug our shoulders and say , "It's human nature." We have lowered our expectations, and have stopped trying to resist lust that leads to sin.

But there are three problems with the sin produced by lust, and these problems do not go away when we ignore them.

1. Sin hurts other people. A man convinces himself to commit adultery, then divorce his wife. He says, "God won't care." What he cannot see is the agony he is causing the people who most love him: his children and his wife. He is consumed with the ephemeral "happiness" that he dreams of having with the other woman. Sin hurts people whom God loves, and that is one reason God does not tolerate it (1 John 4:19-5:2).

2. Sin hurts us. Sin leads to our own destruction. For example, forty years ago, our culture recognized that having sex before marriage was wrong. We called it "shacking up" and "living in sin." Then the sexual revolution happened, and we told each other: "By having sex before marriage, we can find out if we are compatible, and we will be better prepared for marriage." But is this true? We now have enough of a track record with cohabitation to measure how well the experiment has worked. Michael McManus gives the following statistics in his book, *Marriage Savers:*[1]

- 40% of cohabitations break up with no marriage. These couples suffer from traumatic "premarital divorce" because the partners have become "one flesh."
- Cohabiting couples who marry have a 50% higher divorce rate. McManus calls cohabitation "training for divorce."
- Cohabiting couples suffer from household violence about four times more often than married couples. This violence often involves children born out of wedlock.

3. Sin hurts God. God's creation is a beautiful masterpiece. We are, too. Imagine how an artist would feel if he created a beautiful tapestry, but then people used it as a doormat. When people treat each other as doormats, *it hurts God* because it is an abuse of His masterpiece. Because we are created in God's image, He calls us to respect His image in every human being. That is why the Bible says, ultimately, that all sin is against God (Psalm 51:4).

Sanctification

If we wish to love God, we must be willing to deal with deeply ingrained patterns of sin learned before we began to love God. To this end God sends the Holy Spirit, who sensitizes our conscience (2 Corinthians 3:17-18). This process is known as sanctification. Sanctification is a long-term process of tearing out bad habits and replacing them with Christ-like ones. God wants to repair, restore and remodel us as a better house for the Lord to inhabit. But before we get into this process, please pause and do a reality check:

Q2: Do you believe that "deceitful passion" or "lust" has created any bad habits in your life? Is there anything or anyone in your life whom you desire more than God? Are there any patterns of thought, word or deed that your conscience keeps troubling you about? Try to be honest in your prayer journal, even if you do not plan to share your response with the group.

Attaining Virtue

Too little has been written about the rewards of the virtuous life. Virtue is far superior to all other options. Francois Fenelon, the 18th century writer, described well the rewards of virtue:

> Happy are they who give themselves to God! They are delivered from their passions, from the judgments of others, from their malice, from the tyranny of their sayings, from their cold and wretched mocking, from the misfortunes which the world distributes to wealth, from the unfaithfulness and inconstancy of friends, from the wiles and snares of the enemy, from our own weakness, from the misery and brevity of life, from the horrors of a profane death, from the cruel remorse attached to wicked pleasures, and in the end from the eternal condemnation of God.2

Fenelon saw double-mindedness as the most wretched of all options—people trying to be Christians, but still rationalizing sin and resisting conscience. Such people, he said, attain neither the rewards of worldliness, nor the blessings of godliness.

More recently, Leanne Payne writes:

> ...We call people to a radical obedience to Christ. Such obedience requires that we confront, acknowledge, and repent of our sin and propensity toward sin immediately as it becomes conscious. We are thereby spared dreadful suffering, humiliating falls, and perhaps even a lifetime of regret. Too, we discover for ourselves the truth of St.

Paul's words: "No temptation has seized you except what is common to man. And God is faithful; he will not let you be tempted beyond what you can bear. But when you are tempted, he will also provide a way out so that you can stand up under it" (1 Corinthians 10:13).[3]

It is for our own benefit that we pay attention to virtue and holiness, and that we define love as God defines it, not as our culture defines it.

Q3: Recognizing that virtue is not likely to emerge in any of us overnight, are you willing to seek the Holy Spirit to help you attain it? Does it help you to know that the Holy Spirit will teach and counsel you in this, and that you are not alone?

The Pathway to Holiness

The Holy Spirit is in charge of our sanctification, so there is a degree of mystery about how this happens. Sanctification cannot be reduced to six easy steps. I have seen people (like Ruth, whom I mentioned in Chapter Four) be freed from destructive habits in a matter of days, never to struggle with them again.

More often, the Holy Spirit leads us down a pathway that plumbs deeper into our hearts with each passing year, so that we can give ourselves to God at deeper levels. The process of sanctification is rarely an event that "happens to us." It is a cooperative effort between us and God. Usually, the following ingredients are present:

Accepting the truth. To begin with, we have to be willing to receive truth from the word of God. When I first gave my life to Jesus, I had a good start on an addiction to pornography. My conscience was uneasy about porn, yet my culture insisted that there is no harm in it. I was of two minds for a while. Temptation seemed overpowering. Yet as I studied God's word, I came on such passages as Matthew 5:28 and 1 John 2:16, which nailed me to the wall. *I let them nail me.* I didn't go looking for a way to squeak out from under what God was saying. I wanted the truth, I went looking for it, and I accepted it when God gave it to me.

Bringing darkness to light. When things remain hidden, they gain more power to deceive. When I speak out the truth of what I am dealing with, lust begins to lose its power. I learned to confess my sin to a few trusted brothers in Christ, then to my wife, then to my whole congregation, then even to a city-wide church gathering. I believe that people need to see their leaders dealing honestly with private sin, so that they will have the courage to do so, too.

Being accountable to other Christians. It has been a great help to tell other people about my weaknesses, because then they can help protect me and keep me accountable to God's standards. For example, when I signed up for Internet access, I had my Associate Pastor put in the anti-porn software, so that I would not know the password that could deactivate it.

Destroying idols. Sometimes we have to get rid of the source of our temptation. Jesus said that it could feel like we were cutting off a finger or plucking out an eye (Matthew 5:29-30). I eventually realized, for example, that I didn't need the Internet, and so I eventually signed off. It was an idol drawing me away from God.

Q4: Which of the above four ingredients are already a part of your life, and which are not? How could you practically go about adding the ones that are not?

Scripture Study for Chapter Nineteen

- **2 Corinthians 3:17-18** (The Holy Spirit makes us like Jesus.)

- **Matthew 5:27-30** (At times holiness may seem as hard as cutting off a finger!)

- **Matthew 5:43-48** (The goal of sanctification is love.)

- **Matthew 7:13-14** (Sin destroys people. God gives another way.)

- **Romans 6:15-23** (The wages of sin is death.)

- **Romans 6:1-14** (Don't let sin keep on mastering you.)

This is normally how things happen if they are from God.
They start small and grow with the life of God.

20

How Can We Serve Jesus?

One of our greatest needs is the need for significance—a vision that gives us meaning and purpose. The search for significance has taken people, at times, in some tragic and bizarre directions. For example, people have lived and died for these causes:

• A belief that we must get the world ready for a massive visitation of space-ships.

• A belief that, by mass murder and carnage, we can deliver the world from poverty and injustice through Communism.

• A conviction that Nation X is destined to rule the world if only it could get rid of Race Y, which is keeping the nation from its destiny.

•A willingness to let Corporation X manage our lives, dictate our loyalties, interfere with family love, and supplant our worship of God.

Jesus wants to steer us away from such appalling human tragedies. He does this by giving us a calling from God.

Q1: Do you see this search for significance in your own life? Where has it taken you in the past? Has it always led you toward God?

When I sincerely gave my life to Jesus in 1972, He responded by opening up one scripture after another to me, to convince me that my life would have significance if I gave it to Jesus. These verses became His answer to the questions posed in Chapter One:

For we are his workmanship, created in Christ Jesus for good works, which God prepared beforehand, that we should walk in them. (Ephesians 2:10)

Do not be ashamed then of testifying to our Lord...who saved us and called us with a holy calling, not in virtue of our works but in virtue of his own purpose....(2 Timothy 1:8-10)

I began to realize that Jesus had planned specific good works for me to accomplish before I die. He had called me with "a holy calling not in virtue of my works." Paul was saying that we do not decide what our lives are for. God does. We can learn to listen to Jesus, who comes to us and says, "I have a project I would like you to help me with. Could we work on this together?"

A Calling from God

Jesus modeled this kind of life for us. He knew what God the Father was (and wasn't) calling Him to do. When confronted with the Gentiles who needed God's love, He replied that God had sent Him to minister "only to the lost sheep of the house of Israel" (Matthew 15:24). Another time, when Peter demanded that He come back to Capernaum to heal people, He replied, "Let us go to the other towns, for that is why I have come" (Mark 1:35). Jesus knew exactly what He was supposed to accomplish before He died.

"All right," you say, "But He was the Son of God. We're different." But then there's Paul.

Paul also had a clear understanding of what God was calling him to do—to bring the gospel to the Gentiles. Paul spoke of "the field God has assigned to us" (2 Corinthians 10:13) and he didn't want to intrude on someone else's "field." He knew what God wanted him to do. Paul's life was a street with curbs, not a forest full of game trails going every which way. Also, when Paul had completed his God-given calling, he knew it was finished. That is why he wrote,

For I am already on the point of being sacrificed; the time of my departure has come. I have fought the good fight, I have finished the race, I have kept the faith. Henceforth there is laid up for me the crown of righteousness...." (2 Timothy 4:6-8)

Paul, in turn, reminded his protege Timothy "to fan into flame the gift of God, which is in you through the laying on of my hands" (2 Timothy 1:6). After his conversion, Timothy had received a spiritual gift through the laying on of hands. This spiritual gift was an important marker to help Timothy understand God's calling for him, and Paul didn't want Timothy to forget it.

Many other examples of callings can be given. In Augustine's *Confessions,* we learn that his mother Monica prayed incessantly for her son, as Augustine wandered this way and that through New Age religion and then through godless skepticism. Finally, the Spirit of God awakened Augustine to the Bible and Augustine was converted. What is the next thing we read in the *Confessions?* Monica died. Her work was done. God kept her for a purpose. Then He took her to Himself. It was just as Paul wrote:

> If I am to go on living in the body, this will mean fruitful labor for me. Yet what shall I choose? I do not know! I am torn between the two: I desire to depart and be with Christ, which is better by far; but it is more necessary for you that I remain in the body. (Philippians 1:22-24)

Q2: How do you feel about the possibility that God might have a specific work for you to accomplish before you die? Building on your reflections on the questions in Chapter One, do you have any inklings about how, specifically, you can serve Him?

Finding Our Niche

I believe that when we come to Jesus, He will show us a niche, a place in this world where we fit—not a generic one-size-fits-all niche, but a place specifically matched to our talents, personality and abilities, supplemented with spiritual gifts given to do God's Kingdom work.

Some people may say: "But I'm no apostle or great saint. My life is so ordinary. God couldn't have anything special in mind for me." But those "apostles" were nothing but fishermen who themselves would have said, "My life is so ordinary." When Jesus called to them to make them "fishers of men," they were lifted up into an adventure—cooperating with God to do God's projects.

A calling is part of the package plan of the New Covenant (Romans 8:30). Sin has entered into the world to obscure that calling and to blind us from seeing why we were created. But as Jesus wipes away sin from our eyes (as He literally did for Saul of Tarsus—Acts 9:18), we can see His calling more clearly. This is the best answer to our very human need for vision—our vision quest.

Jesus Is the Caller in Every True Calling

What are the principles that will insure that our lives will have significance? How do we get a vision from the Lord? Paul gave us some principles when he spoke of his own vision:

> By the grace God has given me, I laid a foundation as an expert builder, and someone else is building on it. But each one should be careful how he builds. For no one can lay any foundation other than the one already laid, which is Jesus Christ. (1 Corinthians 3:10-11)

All foundations besides Jesus will crumble. If the people I described at the start of this chapter had understood this one simple principle, they might have avoided wasting their lives on doomed causes. Jesus is building a new world with enough vision and significance to satisfy us all. There is a place for us in this kingdom, but to find out what that place is, we must come to Jesus.

Q3: Have you ever specifically asked Jesus to reveal to you how He wants you to serve Him? Why not do it this week?

If It Has Life, It Starts Small

A second point about visions and callings: They are revealed to us in small ways at first, or with unassuming hints and opportunities that do not always seem grandiose. God gives us a chance to be "faithful in a little" before He calls us to be "faithful in much" (Matthew 25:21).

When I arrived at my present church in 1985, one of my members, Karen, was getting her Ph.D. in clinical psychology at Virginia Commonwealth University. In one of my first conversations with her, she said that she sensed the Lord telling her that one day she would minister healing to missionaries. After graduation, the Lord did not open any doors in that direction, but she became head of a crisis response team of our Henrico County Mental Health Center. Yet the conviction that God would eventually move her in the direction of missions never left her.

One day, she was invited to speak at a "Mental Health and Missions" conference. After that, she was invited to speak at other conferences, and to travel overseas to minister to traumatized missionaries. Soon she gained friends in most of the missions organizations in the U.S., who respected the calling on her life. Thirteen years after she first spoke to me about her calling, she resigned from her position with the County and started a totally new concept in Christian ministry—a mobile team that provides crisis response to missionaries in the field. So in thirteen years, I have seen her calling grow from conception to birth.

This is normally how things happen if they are from God. They start small and grow with the life of God.

How God Nurtures His Calling

Third, sooner or later, God confirms His calling in objective ways:

1. You have a deep sense of fulfillment and inner peace when you are doing a particular thing for Jesus; you have a corresponding sense of emptiness when you are not doing it. Other people may not like to do it at all, but when you are doing it, it is supremely fulfilling, even if it involves suffering and stress (2 Corinthians 6:4-10).

2. God confirms His calling either by bringing certain scriptures alive to you or by speaking through other Christians.

3. People encourage you by saying that what you are doing is helpful to them, or helps them to know God better (Matthew 5:16).

4. God confirms His inner guidance by opening up circumstances and making provision.

Most of us do not need a new niche; we only need to have our eyes opened to see the niche God already provided us. Our family. Our neighborhood. Our workplace. Our athletic club or circle of friends. Most vision begins as God shows us how to practice the pattern of Christ right there, the pattern of faith working through love.

Q4: Spend some time in the group telling each other what areas of giftedness you see in each other. Help each other to find your niche in God's kingdom.

Scripture Passages for Chapter Twenty
- **Philippians 1:19-26** (To live is Christ. To die is gain.)

- **John 15:1-11** (Fruitful service begins by coming close to Jesus.)

- **Matthew 25:14-30** (Give to others what Jesus gives you.)

- **2 Timothy 1:8-14** (Paul comes to the end of his calling.)

- **Ephesians 2:1-10** (Saved not *by* good works but *for* good works.)

- **Matthew 4:17-22** (Jesus calls ordinary people.)

Moving in the power of the Holy Spirit is a little like graduating from hand tools to power tools.

21

God's Power
To Do God's Projects

When Jesus chose His first disciples, He turned to a simple fisherman's family. Most of the original twelve were related to Zebedee and his sons. When Jesus broke in upon this family, they discovered that there were unseen demonic enemies to fight, extraordinary spiritual power to wield, a city called New Jerusalem to build, and a world of unimaginably diverse people to invite to a wedding banquet. These fishermen and women were going to be s-t-r-e-t-c-h-e-d!

I believe that Jesus chose simple, ordinary, parochial, unsophisticated, unprofessional people on purpose. He wanted to show all future generations that He could use ordinary men and women in His work. You didn't have to be a Saul of Tarsus—a Pharisee specially trained under the great Gamaliel—to serve God in significant ways.

Still, there was a catch, a caveat, a "whereas." If ordinary people used *ordinary means* to do God's work, they would fail. What made those fisherfolk so effective in serving God was this: they received into themselves the power for ministry that Jesus had received when He was baptized (Acts 10:38), and which Jesus had promised them when He said, "...but remain in the city until you are clothed with power from on high" (Luke 24:48). Jesus promised: "Greater works than these will you do, because I go to the Father" (John 14:12). He was fulfilling the prophecy of Zechariah: "'Not by might nor by power but by my Spirit,' says the Lord Almighty" (4:6).

In both the Old Testament and the New, God says, "Don't rely on the usual political and material methods when building My Kingdom. I have my own ways of building."

Moving in the power of the Holy Spirit is a little like graduating from hand tools to power tools. What are these ways? How can we be effective in serving God?

Learning to Rely on God

To receive the Holy Spirit for empowerment required those fisher folk to learn how to rely on God, not on themselves. This may seem an easy thing, but most of us have to go through several forms of bereavement trauma in learning this. We have to give up:

- Pride of accomplishment; taking credit for what God does. ("I prayed and look what happened. Wow!")
- The security of being in control. ("God, I can't stand surprises, so keep it like it was yesterday.")
- Self-confidence. ("I pretty well know what I'm doing here, God. So you can trust me to handle this one.")
- Patterns of codependency that replace trust in God. ("Sister, I need you to reassure me that I am important.")
- Personal passions and pet peeves. ("God, I just know that you are as ticked off about this as I am.")
- Our right to ease and comfort. ("I'll do whatever you want, God, just as long as....")

The disciples went through the trauma of dying to these patterns while Jesus was still present to help them through it. Then they were on their own—after a fashion. Jesus sent the Holy Spirit, of whom He said,

And I will ask the Father, and he will give you another Counselor to be with you forever—the Spirit of truth. The world cannot accept him, because it neither sees him nor knows him. But you know him, for he lives with you and will be in you. (John 14:16-17

Q1: Do you find it easy to rely on God for anything? Do you find any of the above attitudes getting in the way?

Two Ways of Serving God

As for me, this God-reliant approach to life required a 180° turn-around from what I had learned as a young man with nine years of higher education under my belt.

If you are my age or older, and you are American, you grew up in a culture that put all its confidence in rational knowledge, science and the professions. If anything worthwhile was to be accomplished in this world, it would be done by our educational system. Education was the answer to every problem. All we needed was to study the problem a little more and, bingo, we would be able to solve it.

This confidence in *ourselves* was never questioned in any school I ever attended, even theological school. I do not regret receiving that education. However, the concepts I learned at school were not those Jesus taught. I learned how to do good works *for* God. Jesus taught how to do the works *of* God. In no way are these the same thing.

One unfortunate by-product of professionalism—a result no one intended—was to create a professional clergy, which inadvertently created a nonprofessional class of Christians who were more or less useless. In a professional age, they were not professional. The vast majority of Christians, who did not have time, money or leadings to attend theological school, should not be expected to do much of anything for God, or so we assumed.

I do not believe that this is God's will. He still wants to use fishermen. He wants to give Holy Spirit authorization to people with few credentials, but who are ready to practice the pattern of Christ, faith working through love. People who have learned this pattern have a diploma "written not with ink but with the Spirit of the living God on tablets of human hearts" (2 Corinthians 3:3). They are in a position to do a great deal of good as they let the Holy Spirit use them as ambassadors for Christ.

Q2: Have you ever been led to doubt your usefulness to God? What was behind that doubt? How do you feel about the possibility that the Holy Spirit Himself could give you everything you need to properly serve God? Are you ready to enroll in His school?

The Spirit "upon" and the Spirit "within"

The Bible speaks of two distinct types of spiritual power. The Holy Spirit, as we have seen, works "within" us to change us on the inside, recreating us after the character of Jesus. This is the work of sanctification that we studied in Chapter Nineteen.

But the Bible also says that the Holy Spirit can come "upon" us to use us for specific works that God wants accomplished. The prepositions are significant. We can tell what work of the Holy Spirit is being described anywhere in the Bible by looking at the preposition.[1]

For instance, Paul wrote, "...If anyone does not have the Spirit of Christ, he does not belong to Christ. But if Christ is *in* you, your body is dead because of sin, yet your spirit is alive because of righteousness" (Romans 8:9-10). This passage deals with the Spirit dwelling within us, and it shows that everyone who belongs to Christ has the Holy Spirit. All verses that speak this way are telling us about the inner character-building power of the Spirit of God. (See also 1 Corinthians 6:19-20, John 14:17 for examples of "the Spirit working *within* us.")

On the other hand, wherever the Bible talks about the Holy Spirit falling "upon" people, it is referring to a specific ministry or mighty work of God which follows—a word of prophecy, speaking in tongues, a mighty act of power, an outbreak of worship, a powerfully preached word or a healing. (See Numbers 11:17, 29, John 1:32-33, Luke 4:18 and Acts 1:8 for examples of the Spirit moving "upon" people.) These works of God's Spirit are called spiritual gifts. They are powers God gives us to do good for someone else in Jesus' name.

Acts 8:16 shows us the difference between these two types of power. Philip the evangelist was preaching the word of God in Samaria. Many people came to believe in Jesus and were baptized. We are to understand that they received the Holy Spirit when they accepted Christ and were baptized. But then the word says:

Now when the apostles at Jerusalem heard that Samaria had received the word of God, they sent to them Peter and John, who came down and prayed for them that they might receive the Holy Spirit; for it had not yet fallen *on* any of them, but they had only been baptized in the name of the Lord Jesus. Then they laid their hands on them and they received the Holy Spirit. (Acts 8:14-17, emphasis mine)

This passage has caused many Christians a great deal of bewilderment—"How could they receive the Holy Spirit if they had already received Christ? Are we to think that the Spirit of Christ is different from the Holy Spirit?"

No, but the word here is "on." The Samaritan Christians were becoming equipped for Christian witness and service just as the first disciples had been at the beginning (in Acts 2). In other words, each new generation of Christians must pray for the power of God for its witness and ministry for Jesus.

Balance between Fruit and Gifts

As I have moved among different circles of Christians, I have met many who are familiar with the gifts of the Spirit and the power of God falling "upon" people. To them, a worship service is not complete if there have not been healings, prophecies, people doing carpet time (resting in the power of the Spirit), speaking in tongues, and so on.

There are other circles of Christians who stand against these manifestations of the Holy Spirit, affirming that God wants us to love people, and that Christians should just try to have integrity and be like Jesus.

You see what is happening? One group is saying, "I want the Spirit *within* me, but I'm not crazy about the Spirit coming *upon* me, thank you very much." Others are putting all their hopes on the Spirit coming *upon* them, but hardly pay any attention to what the Spirit wants to do *within* them. They are fascinated with miracles, but could care less about love, patience and faithfulness, let alone self-control!

But the Bible shows a balance between the two. The most famous of all Bible verses was given, in fact, to address this problem of imbalance.

If I speak in the tongues of men and of angels, but have not love, I am only a resounding gong or a clanging cymbal. If I have the gift of prophecy and can fathom all mysteries and all knowledge, and if I have a faith that can move mountains, but have not love, I am nothing. If I give all I possess to the poor and surrender my body to the flames, but have not love, I gain nothing. (1 Corinthians 13:1-4)

In the Bible there is no battle between the fruit of the Spirit (love, joy, peace, patience, kindness, goodness, gentleness, faithfulness and self-control) and the power gifts of the Spirit (like those listed in 1 Corinthians 12:4-7). We need both if we are to be fully equipped for Christian service and witness.

If it is true that God wants a balance between love and spiritual power, let us all seek the part of the equation that we lack.

Some churches are full of mature people—loving, kind, gracious, patient, exemplary in every way—but in whom the power of God for witness and service is not flowing. People like this often insist that they do not need the power of God for ministry. That cannot be true. All of us need both dimensions of the power of God.

Other churches are full of the gifts of the Spirit—but lack the mature fruit of the Holy Spirit. Such people can do a great deal of damage, a problem that we sense was happening at Corinth. People were proud of their spiritual gifts, competed with each other to be the most spiritual, hurt each other with proofs of how spiritual they were and rebelled against leaders like Paul. No humility. No love. No patience.

The mature and seasoned Christian seeks both "the Spirit within" and "the Spirit upon."

Q3: Evaluate yourself. Do you see a balance between these two types of God's power at work in your life? Which would you need to open up to in order to have more of a balance?

Learning To Be Sensitive to the Holy Spirit

How does it work, this reliance on the Holy Spirit? I believe that it is very simple. The hard part is just recognizing that we need the Holy Spirit. Once that hurdle is crossed, it is a matter of learning to recognize His promptings.

For example, Peter and John were walking in Jerusalem one day. On the way to the temple at 3 p.m. they passed a crippled beggar who asked for money. Peter stopped and looked intently at the man. We sense here that the Holy Spirit was speaking to Peter unexpectedly. Peter didn't go out there looking for someone to heal. He responded to some inner prompting, then said to the man, "Look at us." Peter was suddenly being told to challenge this man to stand up on his feet.

The man, staring intently at Peter, began to feel something strange happening inside him. Peter had gripped his attention, and suddenly the awesome majesty of God was between them. Who can explain it? But the result was that the man's legs were re-created by the power of God. This work of power opened the door for Peter to proclaim Jesus to the very people who had just put Jesus to death— the Sanhedrin.

How did all this happen? Peter and the others had spent a good deal of time in prayer, staying close to the Lord, praying that He would send out laborers into the harvest field (Acts 1:14). I don't think that they were trying to be particularly "charismatic." The evidence shows that they were simply going to the temple at the usual time.

But because they were staying close to Jesus, they could hear when Jesus wanted them to do something out of the ordinary. So they were willing to veer off the path to minister to a beggar. The lesson for us here is not, "See if you can lay hands on beggars and heal them." The lesson is: "Stay close to Jesus and He will tell you what He wants." So much of what we do in Jesus' name depends on our learning how to stay close to Jesus.

"Do You Have a Brochure?"

This lesson, of course, applies equally to great miracles and little divine appointments. One time, my wife and I were praying with a prayer team in the top floor of a hotel in Charlotte, North Carolina. The cleaning lady came in at noon to clean our room. We conversed with her, and told her why we were there—to pray. Then my wife said, "Is there anything we could pray for you for?"

The woman, after a pause, responded: "Well, yes. My brother. He's a drug addict and I'm the only one in our family who'll have anything to do with him." We prayed for the boy. She left.

Two minutes later, she knocked on the door again, saying, "Excuse me. Do you have a brochure?"

"A what?" we asked.

"A brochure. Something that tells about who you are." We suddenly realized that our simple prayer had made an impression on her. She wanted to know why we would care enough about her and her brother to pray for them? We told her about Jesus, and referred her to a local church.

We didn't give her any memorized speeches. We just tried to stay sensitive to the Lord. Above all, we practiced the pattern of sound teaching: faith working through love. We went "outside the camp" offering "a sacrifice of praise, the fruit of lips that confess Jesus' name" (Hebrews 13:15).

We don't know what happened to the woman after we prayed for her and her brother—and many occasions of service for Christ end that way. But we are not called only to be the aroma of Christ *to people* anyway, but the aroma of Christ *to God*. The response of the people is of secondary importance. Serving Christ by practicing His pattern out in the world is what is important. We hope, of course, that the woman followed through, went to church as we suggested, and is learning to follow Christ.

Some may ask, how can I receive the power of the Holy Spirit for ministry, and begin to experience God's miracles flowing through me to other people, to bless them? The process is the same one I outlined in Chapter Eight—the "ABC's of faith." Power for Christian service and witness is a promise of the Bible, and we should treat it like any other promise.

A. Ask God to give you His power for Christian service.

B. Believe that He can, and that it is His will to do so.

C. Confess this to be the case. Give Him thanks as He works it out in your life.

D. Do what He says to do—like Peter walking by the Gate Beautiful. Often, it is not until we obey His leadings that we discover the actual evidence of God's power for ministry. (Learning to hear God's prompting may not be easy at first. But we get better at it as we go along.)

How exciting it was when I first began to learn these principles. I was a pastor for a group of students, and was just discovering how to walk with God. As I learned one lesson or another from Jesus, He would give me an opportunity to share it with someone else. Then I had the wonderful reward of knowing that God had just used me to do His work. What joy! What reward!

Q4: Can you relate to this idea that the Holy Spirit could guide you in witnessing to people about Jesus, or in blessing them with His love?

Scriptures for Chapter Twenty-One

- **2 Corinthians 5:16-21** (The calling to be ambassadors for Christ)

- **2 Corinthians 5:11-15** (The motive for Christian service: the love of Christ)

- **Luke 24:44-49** (The power of the Holy Spirit is required if we are to truly be Christ's witnesses.)

- **Acts 3:1-10** (Peter trusts the Holy Spirit in his Christian witness.)

- **Acts 8:4-17** (The Holy Spirit draws the Samaritans to Jesus, and then equips them with power for ministry.)

- **1 Corinthians 12:1-11** (The Holy Spirit draws us to Jesus and equips us with power for ministry.)

Though He didn't agree with their doctrine, was grieved by their morals and hurt by their hate, Jesus loved the lost sheep of the house of Israel to the end.

22

The Pattern of Sound Teaching

The dynamics of faith working through love can be compared to a pool of water. With every pool of fresh water, there is an inflow and an outflow. God has provided the way for the human heart to be continually refreshed and renewed. But this can happen only if we have the proper inflow and outflow. God's inflow is Christian faith. God's outflow is Christian love.

No Faith, No Love

Several "heart-conditions" can prevent this continual refreshing of our hearts. The first is that we shall have neither inflow nor outflow. As the prophet Jeremiah wrote, some people have forsaken "the spring of living water and have dug their own cisterns that cannot hold water" (Jeremiah 2:13). They have not learned to open either the faith channel toward God or the love channel toward other people. Their lives become stagnant.

Such people are always on the lookout for something new, because they know that they are not satisfied. They may look for new jobs, new spouses, new recreation, new projects, new playmates—the list goes on. All these are what Henri Nouwen called "protective distractions." Such people may appear to be the life of the party wherever they go. Yet when they are alone, they are confronted by the stagnancy within. The very fervency with which they fling themselves into jocularity betrays their inner desperation.

Christians are not immune to this stagnancy. For one reason or another, we can close off both the inflow and the outflow, despite having the name of Christian. But when stagnancy intrudes, we can at least recognize that it comes from cutting off the channels of faith and love—and we can re-open whatever channels we have closed.

Q1: Have you ever struggled with boredom or stagnancy? Have you seen this as a spiritual condition—or as a problem to be solved with non-spiritual solutions, such as electronic gadgets, computer games or a steady diet of movies or soap operas?

Love without Faith

Second, there are those who try to love, but who do not have faith to feed their love. Invariably, their love is betrayed, misunderstood, ridiculed—and succumbs to evil. Then we discover this truth: Apart from Jesus we can do nothing (John 15:5). How is it possible to love the unlovable? Or to forgive the unforgivable? Without faith to fill our emptiness, love slows to a trickle, then dries up altogether.

I experienced this drying up of love during the social activism of the 1960's, which began in a desire for love and justice. How well I remember the idealism of youth—students who were willing to sacrifice their own peace and security because of what they believed in. The young were trying two bold experiments in love and justice: the Haight-Ashbury flower-children and the Berkeley peace marches. "Make love, not war" was the slogan of the times.

Yet both experiments ended in tragedy. The Flower Children discovered mind-altering drugs and free sex. The horrors implicit in that lifestyle became apparent within two years. "Something is missing here," I said to myself, as I observed the debacle.

As for the student activists: I remember going back home one summer to Madison, Wisconsin, where I had grown up. I returned to the haunts of my youth at the University of Wisconsin. How Madison had changed! Businesses were all boarded up because activist students chanting "Make love, not war," had trashed everything. They had even dynamited one of the campus buildings. My favorite pizza house had been moved into a fortress-like building with no windows so that the business could protect itself from these "loving" students. What blindness had overcome the young! They could not see that they were not practicing love. They needed to know God, who is love. They (we) needed to know about the inflow.

Many married couples experience this same drying up of love. They cling to a wistful desire for romance, yet the springs of romance run dry in a month. Countless couples have had to discover how to start the inflow of faith to replenish their love, as Dr. Everett Worthington and I have described in our book, *Value Your Mate.*[1] Faith in Christ can open up those springs more bountifully than ever. Sometimes God takes away every reason for practicing love except one: to do it for Jesus.

Q2: Do you recall times when you tried to love some person (or a group, culture or race of people) who were difficult to love? How might faith in Christ help in such situations?

Faith without Love

Third, some of us have an inflow of faith, but not the outflow of love. Their faith rises very fast and boils over in a burst of fanaticism, as it did during the Crusades against the Moslems in the Middle Ages (which were, in turn, a reaction against the violence of Islamic Caliphs who had killed Christians by the thousands).

During the last dozen years, I have studied the first encounters between white people and natives in the American West. It is a tragic story. In many cases God prepared the way of Christ by speaking to tribal leaders about the Savior. In the 18th century, the Spokans, Kalispels, Coeur d'Alenes and Flatheads received prophecy that God had sent a Savior into the world. They called Him The Master of Life because they didn't know His name.

The Kalispels and the Flatheads knew that this person was somehow connected with a cross, which they recognized as a powerful talisman that would protect them. But they didn't know the meaning of the cross.

The Coeur d'Alenes, as I have said, were already celebrating Christmas by the middle of the 18th century.

The Spokans had been told to look for "leaves bound together, carried by people of white skin, out of which God would come"—a prophecy about the Bible. When white traders brought Bibles, tribal leaders recognized them to be the fulfillment of tribal prophecy. Most of these people, during the 1820's, begged the whites to send missionaries to them, so that they could learn of the Master of Life. They were beginning to know His name: Jesus.

White people did send missionaries during the 1840's. But when they came, they often preached hellfire and damnation, not the love of God. Many could not bring themselves to honor native lifeways, dismissing them simply as "pagan." Few if any listened to native tribal leaders for the ways that God had already spoken into tribal culture about His Son. Some even took over Indian land, profiting from injustices perpetrated by non-Christian white people. There were some Christians who had the whole pattern together, but the majority had not found the connector between faith and love.

I have come to one conclusion: We Christians can pick and choose parts of the pattern of Christ and leave the rest alone. We can open our lives to one part, and refuse to see the other parts. Those missionaries had the faith part, but they didn't have the love part. Their desire to be missionaries, apparently, was motivated by something other than the love of God for the people they served. It is a bitter lesson, but one that we must face up to. Faith without love presents Christ in a way that He doesn't deserve to be presented.

When we see that our neighbors resent our Christianity, it may not be because they are serving the devil, or have anti-Christian attitudes or hardness of heart against God. Their resistance may be the expected result of our lack of love, or the lovelessness of other Christians who have gone before us. What are we giving to unbelievers that would make them want our faith? Are we seeking ways to bless them? Are we praying that *God* would bless them?

Q3: Do you see any times or seasons in your life when you have tried to share faith without demonstrating a corresponding love? Have you seen others do this, and what have you learned from their example?

God's Culture Invades Ours

God's aim, as I have described it in *Fresh Bread,* is to get the faith and love flowing freely and in the right directions. When this happens, we can become a powerful force that changes the world— at least, we can change whatever part of the world our lives touch.

To keep us on track, we have only to keep our eyes on Jesus who always modeled for us the pattern He recommended. He lived a life of obedient faith, discerning what the Father wanted, and trusting Him for the outcome. His prayer in the Garden of Gethsemane "Not my will, but yours," demonstrates this principle of faith, even to giving up His life.

What was the outcome of this sacrifice of faith in God's fatherly care? Love—for the very people who crucified Him. Though He didn't agree with their doctrine, was grieved by their morals, and hurt by their hatred, Jesus was called to love the lost sheep of the house of Israel to the end.

Now He calls us to take up our cross and follow Him. And in the absence of Roman centurions and angry mobs, this command translates into a pattern we can live out each day of our lives: faith working through love.

Give What You Received

This twenty-two week Bread group is at an end. It would be a good time to reflect on what you have gained from it.

Q4: Looking back on the journey the group has taken together, how has God worked to change your life? Have you received anything of value from the group? Try to enumerate these things on paper and share with the group.

The Bible says that we should give others what we have received. When we do, the blessing of God's gifts grows. On the other hand, when we bury our gifts in the ground, we lose what we were given.

Let the group discuss how you can give others what you have received in the group. Pray about these things before any final group decisions are made about continuing or disbanding the group. Some options to pray about:

•Let the group divide and form new Bread groups, attracting other people drawn from neighborhoods or workplaces. Several people in the present group can become leaders of the new groups. They should order my *Bread Group Leader's Guide* (available from Bethlehem Books).

•Couples can learn to apply the faith-working-through-love principle to their marriage, using my book, *Value Your Mate* (available from Baker Book House at your local book store, or from Bethlehem Books). Two or more couples can come together to form a twelve-week Value Your Mate group.

•Continue to meet as a group, using another discipleship guide, such as *Food Groups: A Balanced Diet for Christian Growth* (available from Bethlehem Books).

•Seek private, personal ways of sharing your faith and love with others. Disband as a group, at least for a season.

Scripture Study for Chapter Twenty-two

- **1 Timothy 1:3-7** (Love, a pure heart and a good conscience coming from sincere faith)

- **1 Timothy 4:6-16** (The pattern is of value both for this life and the life to come.)

- **2 Timothy 1:8-14** (The pattern of sound teaching: faith and love together)

- **2 Peter 1:3-11** (The pattern of Christ begins with faith and ends in love.)

- **Galatians 5:1-6** (Faith working or expressing itself in love)

- **Titus 3:1-11** (Attend to the pattern. Avoid stupidities.)

Notes

Chapter One
1. Doug Murren, *The Baby Boomerang* (Ventura, California: Regal, 1990), 155.
2. *The Presbyterian Outlook*, February 3, 1997, 5. Quote is from The Index of Leading Spiritual Indicators.

Chapter Two
1. D. T. Niles, *Who Is This Jesus?* (Nashville: Abingdon, 1968), 121.
2. Zeb Bradford Long and Douglas McMurry, *The Collapse of the Brass Heaven* (Grand Rapids: Chosen, 1994), 55-56.
3. Abul A'la Mawdudi, *Towards Understanding Islam* (Salimiah, Kuwait, International Islamic Federation of Student Organizations, 1986), 38.
4. Daniel Yankelovich, "New Rules In American Life," *Psychology Today*, Vol. 15, No.4, 68-69.
5. Otto Friedrich, "Cheating by the millions," *Time*, March 28, 1983, 33.
6. Roland Bainton, *Here I stand: A Life of Martin Luther.* (Nashville: Abingdon, 1950), 65.

Chapter Three
1. Josephus, *Antiquities* 18.3.3.
2. *Presbyterian Global Prayer Digest*, Vol. 17, No. 4, April, 1998, 9.
3. *The Christian Witness*, Vol. 1, #1, December, 1997. Quotes are from Samaveda, Thadiyamaha Brahmanam.
4. *Ibid, 1.*
5. *Ibid, 1.*
6. Joseph Seltice, *Saga of the Coeur D'Alene Indians* (Fairfield, Washington, Ye Galleon, 1990), 16-19.
7. I have listed the sources for my research in *The Collapse of the Brass Heaven* (Grand Rapids: Chosen, 1994), 265.

Chapter Four
1. I have long since lost the original source for this testimony but I believe it came from Campus Crusade for Christ.

Chapter Five
1. "A Call To Do Evangelism," Report by Brad Long, 3-4.
2. Archibald Alexander, *The Log College* (London: Banner of Truth, 1851, 1968), 99-102. The story of William Tennent's experience of heaven is three pages long.
3. Bilquis Sheikh with Richard H. Schneider, *I Dared To Call Him Father* (Old Tappan, NJ: Chosen, 1978), 66-67.

Chapter Six

1. The Nicene Creed. The Apostles' Creed also affirmed this hope.

2. Sigmund Freud, *The Future of an Illusion* (New York: Liveright, 1928), 95.

3. Reinhold Niebuhr, *Moral Man and Immoral Society* (New York: Charles Scribner's Sons, 1932, 1960), 82.

4. Alexander Dumas, *Short Stories* (New York: Walter J. Black, 1927), 22.

5. Zeb Bradford Long & Douglas McMurry, *The Collapse of the Brass Heaven* (Grand Rapids: Chosen, 1994), 110-122.

6. The book of Revelation is not a continuous account of the end times, as many suppose, but distinct visions that each focus on a different part of God's world: the Church, world history, nature, spiritual conflict, the triumph of righteousness, the kingship of Jesus, and God's New Creation.

7. The "title deed" interpretation of the scroll follows J. Vernon McGee, *Revelling Through Revelation, Vol. I* (Pasadena: Thru the Bible, 1962), 45.

Chapter Eight

1. John Calvin, *The Institutes of the Christian Religion III.20.2.*

2. Martha Williamson and Robin Sheets, *Touched By An Angel: Stories from the Hit Television Series* (Grand Rapids: Zondervan, 1997), 186. John Dye plays the angel of death in the TV series.

Chapter Nine

1. Richard Foster and James Bryan Smith, *Devotional Classics* (San Francisco: Harper, 1993), 340. Quote is from *What Shall This Man Do?*

2. Foster, Smith, 341.

3. C.S. Lewis, *Letters To Malcolm: Chiefly On Prayer* (New York: Harcourt, Brace, Jovanovich, 1964), 22.

Chapter Eleven

1. "He that has ears to hear, let him hear" (Luke 14:35).

2. *Devotional Classics*, 95. Henri Nouwen, *Making All Things New.*

3. *Devotional Classics*, 2-3.

Chapter Twelve

1. Brad Long and I have elaborated on these stages of prayer in our book, *Prayer That Shapes the Future* (Grand Rapids: Zondervan, 1999).

Chapter Fourteen

1. Michael E. McCullough, Steven J. Sandage and Everett L. Worthington, Jr., *To Forgive Is Human* (Downers Grove, Illinois: InterVarsity, 1997), 60.

2. Jonathan Goforth, *By My Spirit*, Reprint #51 (Newton, Kansas: Herald Of His Coming, 1993), 9.

Chapter Fifteen
1. Dennis and Matthew Linn, *Healing Life's Hurts* (New York: Paulist Press, 1978), 2.

Chapter Sixteen
1. Zeb Bradford Long and Douglas McMurry, *Prayer That Shapes the Future* (Grand Rapids: Zondervan, 1999), page numbers not available at this time.

2. Max Delespesse, *Christian Community: Leaven and Lifestyle* (Ottawa: Saint Paul University, 1968), 41.

3. Delespesse, 42.

Chapter Seventeen
1. *The Presbyterian Outlook,* Feb. 3, 1997, 5. Quotes are from George Barna's *The Index of Leading Spiritual Indicators.*

2. Sally Morgenthaler, *Worship Evangelism* (Grand Rapids: Zondervan, 1995), 59. She quotes George Gallup, *Religion In America, 1992-3.*

3. *Christianity Today,* 27:7, April 8, 1983, 56-57.

4. George Barna, *Understanding Ministry in a Changing Culture* (Glendale, California, Barna Research Group, 1993), 90.

Chapter Eighteen
1. *The Theological Dictionary of the New Testament,* Vol 1 Gerhard Kittel, ed., (Grand Rapids: Eerdmans. 1964), 37.

2. Roland Bainton, *Here I Stand* (Nashville: Abingdon, 1950), 262.

Chapter Nineteen
1. Michael J. McManus, *Marriage Savers* (Grand Rapids: Zondervan, 1995), 38-41.

2. Richard J. Foster and James Bryan Smith, *Devotional Classics* (San Francisco: Harper Collins, 1993), 47. Excerpt is from *Christian Perfection.*

3. Leanne Payne, *Restoring the Christian Soul* (Grand Rapids: Baker, 1991), 20.

Chapter Twenty-one
1. Brad Long and I elaborate on this principle of the Holy Spirit's work in our book, *Receiving the Power* (Grand Rapids: Chosen, 1997).

Chapter Twenty-two
1. Douglas McMurry and Everett Worthington, *Value Your Mate* (Grand Rapids: Baker, 1993).

To order additional copies of

Fresh Bread:
How Jesus Draws Us to God

send $10.00 plus $3.95 shipping and handling to:

Books, Etc.
P.O. Box 1406
Mukilteo, WA 98275

or have your credit card ready and call:

(800) 917-BOOK
Quantity discounts available

Fresh Bread and the Bread groups have been adopted by Presbyterian and Reformed Renewal Ministries International (PRRMI), for their Philip Endeavor. PRRMI is an interdenominational and international community of believers in Jesus who work for the renewal of Christians and churches by the power of the Holy Spirit and God's word. The Philip Endeavor is the evangelistic thrust of that ministry, spreading the good news of how Jesus Christ draws us to God. *Fresh Bread, The Bread Group Leader's Guide* and *Food Groups: A Balanced Diet for Christian Growth* may be ordered from PRRMI:

PRRMI
PO BOX 429
BLACK MOUNTAIN, NC 28711
828-669-7373
FAX 828-669-4880
www.prrmi.org

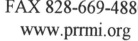

Bethlehem Books

publishes and distributes books by Douglas McMurry
that promote Christian disciple-making.
Available in 1999:

Fresh Bread: (WinePress, 1999) $10.00

Bread Group Leader's Guide (Bethlehem, 1998). $4.00

Food Groups (Bethlehem, 1986). $6.00
Intensive Bible study on the three ingredients of basic Christianity: faith, love and holiness.

Value Your Mate (Baker, 1993) $8.00
Co-authored with Dr. Everett Worthington, this book applies the pattern of faith working through love to eight dimensions of marriage.

The Collapse of the Brass Heaven (Chosen, 1994). . . $12.00
Co-authored with Brad Long, this book shows why Western societies have lost God's power and blessing, and how we can get them back.

Receiving the Power (Chosen, 1997) $12.00
Co-authored with Brad Long, this book helps people open up to the power of the Holy Spirit. Following the tradition of R.A. Torrey and his grandson, Archer Torrey, it seeks to avoid simplistic concepts about the Holy Spirit that have been divisive to the Body of Christ.

Prayer That Shapes the Future (Zondervan, May, 1999)
Co-authored with Brad Long, this book shows how prayer births into the future what does not yet exist.

Bethlehem Books
2508 Dickens Rd.
Richmond, VA 23230

Phone: (804) 282-4872
Fax: (804) 285-9430